SMALL BATCH BAKES

Edd Kimber

SMALL BATCH BAKES

Edd Kimber
@THEBOYWHOBAKES

PHOTOGRAPHY BY EDD KIMBER

KYLE BOOKS

Introduction

The old adage that good things come in small packages should be the motto of this book. The recipes that appear in these pages are the definition of both good and small. Baking is so often thought of as something we do for large gatherings, for birthday parties, holidays and special occasions. This book is for the times and those people where smaller serving sizes are needed. That could be because you have ingredients left over, but not enough to use in other larger recipes; because you live alone but enjoy baking regularly and don't like waste; because you're a student and your budget doesn't stretch to the ingredients needed for big baking projects; because you want a dessert for date night; or maybe because you just like baking for you and the kids. Small batch baking is, for me, all about the joys of baking, but in amounts that mean I can bake more often and not have to worry about leftovers.

Within this book are recipes that make just one cookie, desserts for date night that serve two, recipes that make four servings when you might want a weeknight dessert, and a few recipes that serve small gatherings of six. Alongside the sweet stuff there is also a sprinkling of savoury – think pizza dough, brioche burger buns, sausage hand pies and quiche.

It is also worth noting that many of these recipes can be frozen, so any leftovers can be kept for a later date. This means that even if you're baking just for yourself, every recipe is suitable for small households.

With small batch baking you will often come across the issue of recipes needing a single egg white or egg yolk, or only half a batch of pastry. To prevent waste and to help you find ideas for using up those leftovers, this book includes lists of recipes that make use of those whites and yolks (see page 12). Everything in the Small Batch Basics chapter has a relatively long shelf life, and the resulting recipes freeze well, so ultimately nothing should go to waste.

COOK'S NOTES

- UK weights and terminology are followed by US equivalents in brackets.
- All spoon measures are level.
- All eggs are large (or extra large in the US) and preferably free-range.
- All vegetables (including garlic) are medium-sized and should be peeled or trimmed.
- All herbs and leaves should be washed and trimmed, as necessary.
- Sea salt and freshly ground black pepper should be used wherever seasoning is required.

Ingredients

When it comes to small batch baking and the ingredients used, there isn't anything different from traditional baking, right? Actually, no – there are a few differences to bear in mind. Much of what is bought specifically for baking is designed for certain portion sizes. Yeast, for example, most frequently comes in individual 7g packets, which are used for a loaf based on 500g (1lb 2oz) of flour – not very helpful if you're using only ½ teaspoon of yeast in a recipe. Lots of other ingredients come in cans that, once opened, need decanting into other containers. Because of this I have a few tips for the small batch baker...

CANS

Instead of buying ingredients such as dulce de leche or condensed milk in cans, I buy them in bottles or glass jars, which are easier to reseal and store in the refrigerator for future use. Resealable packaging is generally preferable to cans, so look out for other items that use it.

YEAST

Trying to store partially used packets of yeast is downright annoying, so I recommend buying yeast that comes in small resealable containers (generally available in supermarkets alongside packet yeast) and measuring out the required amount yourself. Apart from being cheaper and using less packaging, it's less wasteful.

FRUIT

Leftover fruit is another issue when baking in small batch style because the packaged amounts are sometimes more than required. Of course, you can simply eat the fruit as it stands, but there are other options. If I have leftover berries, for example, or maybe lemons that need using up, I will make a single jar of jam or lemon curd (see pages 164 and 162). If you don't have enough leftover fruit for a recipe, the best option is to freeze it, using a method called 'flash freezing'. This involves placing the fruit on a parchment-lined tray, ensuring the individual pieces aren't touching, and freezing until solid. The fruit can then be transferred to a freezer bag and stored for up to a month.

Freezing

Basics

Within this book you'll find recipes that make from one to six servings, but even if you don't need the full amount, it is still worth making as most baked items freeze really well. Cakes can be frozen for up to a month, but any frosting or buttercream accompaniment should be frozen separately. Once defrosted, you might find the topping or filling needs beating to smooth it out, and that it loses a little volume in the process, but it tastes absolutely fine.

Bread is especially freezer friendly and always useful to have on hand. Homemade bread will freeze for at least a month. Pastry trimmings too can be saved for future use; simply gather them gently into a ball, then flatten and cover in clingfilm (plastic wrap) and freeze until needed. They can be used in recipes that require only a small amount of pastry, such as the Matcha Cheesecake Tarts on page 29.

The final chapter of this book provides what I think of as foundation recipes – small batch basics, such as pastry, brioche dough and jam. The pastry recipes tend to make a little more than you'll need for a single recipe, but that is deliberate because it is easier to work with a slightly larger amount of ingredients, and the extra can be frozen for another day (you'll thank yourself later). Pastry keeps for at least a month in the freezer and the quality remains incredibly high. Refrigerated pastry keeps for 3–4 days.

As some of the recipes in this book don't use a full quantity of the basics, each of the basic recipes includes a list of recipes in which you can use up any leftovers.

Equipment

For small batch baking you need the usual standard items, such as bowls and cooling racks. I also use a 15 x 5cm (6 x 2in) round cake tin, 10cm (4in) loose-bottomed tart tins, 250ml (9fl oz) ovenproof ramekins, a 23 x 13cm (9 x 5in) loaf tin and a mini bundt tin. However, there are a few other items that are especially helpful when baking small.

BUTTER WARMER/MILK PAN

These two small pans are extremely useful. The butter warmer is a mini pan, about 8cm (3in) in diameter, and can be used for all manner of tasks, such as melting small amounts of chocolate and warming small amounts of leftover custards and sauces, as well as for melting butter. Milk pans are about 15cm (6in) in diameter and, apart from heating milk, are perfect for making small batches of choux pastry or sauces, or for setting up as a bain-marie (double boiler).

HAND-HELD MIXER

Stand mixers, such as KitchenAids and Kenwoods, are not designed for small batch bakes, so whipping a single egg white in one of these machines is not all that effective. However, a hand-held mixer, the type with two detachable beaters, is the perfect tool for small batch baking. It is also significantly cheaper than a stand mixer. One drawback of the hand-held mixer is that it's not great for making bread dough, even when manufacturers claim it is, so I would advise making bread recipes by hand, or with a sturdy stand mixer if you have one.

MINI SPATULAS/WOODEN SPOONS

My kitchen is overflowing with spatulas and wooden spoons in a wide range of sizes, but I always opt for small ones when working with small batches of ingredients, as the standard ones can be a little cumbersome.

MINI BALLOON WHISK/SAUCE WHISK

While a big balloon whisk is a standard item in many kitchens, it may not be the most effective tool for all small batch tasks. I often find a mini balloon whisk or a small sauce whisk more effective, especially for anything prone to clumping or going lumpy.

SMALL BAKING TRAY/EIGHTH SHEET PAN

For most of the recipes in this book the exact size of baking tray is not important; you can use what you already have. However, for some small batch recipes, such as the Chocolate and Espresso Brioche Buns or the Cacio e Pepe Stuffed Rolls (see pages 123 and 140) a small rimmed baking tray – known in the US as an eighth sheet pan – is the ideal size and style. These trays, which measure about 23 x 15cm (9 x 6in), have a rim all round and are perfect for recipes that need containing. This makes them suitable for breads, but also for small sheet cakes, such as Vegan Baked Alaska (see page 112).

SIX-HOLE MUFFIN TRAY

If you already have a standard 12-hole muffin tray, there is no need to buy a smaller one. However, if you're starting from scratch and storage is an issue in your kitchen, a 6-hole tray is all you'll need for small batch baking.

SMALL OFFSET SPATULAS

I recommend offset spatulas for every style of baking, but they are especially useful when baking small. They are great for spreading batters into even layers and for decorating cakes.

ELECTRONIC SCALES

Accuracy is always important in baking, but even more so when baking small batches, so I always advise baking by weight to ensure the correct result. The only recipe where this doesn't hold true is the Emergency Chocolate Chip Cookie (see page 50), where measuring spoons are used instead. Electronic scales are cheap and easy to use, and because they can be zeroed between each weighed ingredient, they also mean less washing up.

Leftover Eggs

Leftover egg whites and egg yolks need never go to waste. The whites can be frozen in ice-cube trays, then transferred to plastic bags and stored in the freezer for up to three months. Alternatively, they can be kept in a sealed container in the refrigerator for up to four days. Egg yolks can also be stored in the refrigerator in this manner, but they need to be covered in water to prevent them from drying out.

Leftover egg yolks can also be used instead of a whole beaten egg for eggwash, simply whisk them with a splash of milk or cream before use. Egg yolks can also be used to seal a blind-baked pastry case.

The following recipes use egg yolks or egg whites (sometimes in addition to whole eggs) and are a great way to use up any you might have left over.

PASTRY

Egg Custard Tarts

MAKES 4

While Portuguese custard tarts might take the award for most fashionable, the less trendy English egg custard tart deserves equal praise. Its custard, rich with egg yolk, is delicately flavoured and topped with a generous grating of nutmeg. If I have anything close to a Proustian connection with a dish, this may be the one, a joyful reminder of my childhood with every bite.

½ batch Sweet Pastry (see page 152)

Flour, for dusting

1 egg yolk, beaten (optional)

Freshly grated nutmeg

FOR THE FILLING

120ml (4fl oz/½ cup) double (heavy) cream

120ml (4fl oz/½ cup) whole milk

2 teaspoons vanilla bean paste

4 large egg yolks

50g (1¾oz/¼ cup) caster (superfine or granulated) sugar

Cut the pastry into 4 equal slices. Lightly flour the work surface and roll each piece of pastry into a circle about 3mm (⅛in) thick. Use to line four 10cm (4in) loose-bottomed tart tins (or small brioche moulds, if you want a more modern look), trimming off any excess pastry. Refrigerate the tart cases for 1 hour, until firm.

Preheat the oven to 200°C (180°C Fan) 400°F, Gas Mark 6. Line each tart case with a crumpled piece of parchment paper, fill with baking beans or rice and place on a baking tray (cookie sheet). Bake for about 20 minutes, or until the edges are lightly browned. Remove the parchment and beans, then bake for a further 5 minutes, or until the inside of the pastry is golden. To ensure the pastry remains crisp after filling, you can brush beaten egg yolk inside the tart cases and bake them for a minute or two more to create a barrier that helps prevent a soggy base. Set aside and lower the oven temperature to 140°C (120°C Fan) 275°F, Gas Mark 1.

To make the filling, place the cream, milk and vanilla in a small saucepan and bring to a simmer. Meanwhile, whisk together the egg yolks and sugar. Pour over the cream mixture, whisking as you do so to prevent the yolks from scrambling.

Return the tart cases to the oven, then carefully fill each one with the custard; they should be very full, so filling them in the oven prevents spillage. Grate over a generous amount of nutmeg and bake for about 20 minutes, or until the custard is set around the edges with a gentle wobble in the middle. Set aside and cool to room temperature before transferring to the refrigerator for 2 hours.

Carefully unmould the custard tarts and serve. They are best on the day they are made, but can be served up to 2 days later.

Rhubarb and Raspberry Frangipane Tarts

MAKES 4

Frangipane, an almond paste perhaps best known for its use in Bakewell tart, is wonderfully adaptable. Pistachios, pecans, hazelnuts or whichever nuts you prefer can be used instead of almonds. Got some leftover pastry cream? You can fold it through the frangipane to make a lighter version. Frangipane can also be used to make almond croissants, galette des rois or another brunch favourite, the bostock (frangipane topped brioche). In this recipe, a crisp pastry case is lined with raspberry jam, topped with almond frangipane and finished with rhubarb and flaked almonds.

½ batch Sweet Pastry (see page 152)

Flour, for dusting

4 tablespoons raspberry jam, shop-bought or homemade (see page 164)

FOR THE FRANGIPANE

50g (1¾oz/3½ tablespoons) unsalted butter, at room temperature

50g (1¾oz/¼ cup) caster (superfine or granulated) sugar

1 large egg

70g (2½oz/¾ cup) ground almonds

1–2 drops almond extract

FOR THE TOPPING

100g (3½oz) rhubarb, cut into 2.5cm (1in) pieces

20g (¾oz/3 tablespoons) flaked almonds

Demerara sugar, for sprinkling

Cut the pastry into 4 equal slices. Lightly flour a work surface and roll each piece of pastry into a circle about 3mm (⅛in) thick. Use to line 4 x 10cm (4in) loose-bottomed tart tins, trimming off any excess. Refrigerate for at least 1 hour.

Preheat the oven to 200°C (180°C Fan) 400°F, Gas Mark 6.

Line each tart case with a crumpled piece of parchment paper, fill with baking beans or rice and place on a baking tray (cookie sheet). Bake for about 20 minutes, or until the edges are lightly browned. Remove the parchment and beans, then bake for a further 5 minutes, or until the pastry is golden. Set aside and lower the oven temperature to 180°C (160°C Fan) 350°F, Gas Mark 4.

To make the frangipane, beat the butter and sugar together in a bowl until light and fluffy. Add the egg and beat to combine. Add the ground almonds and almond extract and beat once more.

Place a tablespoon of jam in each pastry case and spread evenly. Spoon in the frangipane and spread evenly over the jam. Top the frangipane with the rhubarb, a few flaked almonds and a sprinkling of demerara sugar.

Bake for 25–30 minutes, or until the frangipane and almonds are lightly browned. These tarts are best eaten on the day they are made, but will keep for about 3 days if stored in a sealed container.

Blueberry Cream Tarts

MAKES 4

Think of these delicious creations as a slight twist on classic fruit tarts. Instead of the usual sweet pastry filled with pastry cream, these are made with incredibly flaky pastry that shatters when cut into, and a vanilla-rich custard lightened with a little whipped cream, making it taste almost like ice cream. I like to use blueberries, but you can use any type of fruit you fancy.

½ batch Flaky Pastry (see page 154)

Flour, for dusting

1 egg yolk, beaten (optional)

200g (7oz) blueberries

Lemon zest, for sprinkling (optional)

FOR THE FILLING

½ batch Pastry Cream (see page 161)

80ml (3fl oz/⅓ cup) double (heavy) cream

Cut the pastry into 4 equal slices. Lightly flour a work surface and roll each piece of pastry into a circle about 3mm (⅛in) thick. Use to line 4 x 10cm (4in) loose-bottomed tart tins, trimming off any excess. Refrigerate for at least 1 hour.

Preheat the oven to 200°C/180°C Fan, 400°F, Gas Mark 6.

Line each pastry case with a piece of crumpled parchment paper, fill with baking beans or rice and place on a baking tray (cookie sheet). Bake for about 20 minutes, or until the edges are lightly browned. Remove the parchment and beans, then bake for a further 5 minutes, or until the inside of the pastry is golden. To ensure it remains crisp after filling, you can brush beaten egg yolk inside the tart cases and bake them for a minute or two more to create a barrier that helps prevent a soggy base. Set aside until cool.

To make the filling, beat the pastry cream until smooth. In a separate bowl, whisk the double cream until it's holding soft peaks. Fold this cream, a third at a time, into the pastry cream. Spoon the filling into the tart cases and top with the blueberries and lemon zest (if using).

Once assembled, serve the tarts within a few hours, before the pastry has a chance to soften. If you want to serve later, store the unfilled tart cases in a sealed container, and refrigerate the filling until needed.

NOTE If you would like to make these tarts with sweet pastry, see the recipe on page 152, and bake in the same way as the Egg Custard Tarts on page 16.

Lemon Poppy Seed Meringue Tarts

MAKES 4

Lemon poppy seed muffins are a true classic, so why not use that ingredient combo in the form of lemon meringue tarts? Poppy seeds are incorporated into the flaky pastry, and the filling is my homemade lemon curd, which is a thicker and creamier version than shop-bought, and perfect as a filling for a tart or cake. The final touch is a topping of Swiss meringue.

½ batch Flaky Pastry (see page 154), adding 2 tablespoons poppy seeds just before the water

Flour, for dusting

1 egg yolk, beaten (optional)

1 batch Lemon Curd (see page 162)

FOR THE SWISS MERINGUE TOPPING

1 large egg white

75g (2¾oz/½ cup + 2 tablespoons) caster (superfine or granulated) sugar

1 teaspoon vanilla bean paste

Cut the pastry into 4 equal slices. Lightly flour a work surface and roll each piece of pastry into a circle about 3mm (⅛in) thick. Use to line 4 x 10cm (4in) loose-bottomed tart tins, trimming off any excess. Refrigerate for at least 1 hour.

Preheat the oven to 200°C (180°C Fan) 400°F, Gas Mark 6.

Line each pastry case with a piece of crumpled parchment paper, fill with baking beans or rice and place on a baking tray (cookie sheet). Bake for about 20 minutes, until the edges are lightly browned. Remove the parchment and beans, then bake for a further 5 minutes, or until the inside of the pastry is golden. To ensure it remains crisp after filling, you can brush beaten egg yolk inside the tart cases and bake them for a minute or two more to create a barrier that helps prevent a soggy base. Set aside until cool.

Spoon the lemon curd into the pastry cases and spread evenly. Refrigerate while you prepare the topping.

Place the egg white and sugar in a heatproof bowl set over a pan of simmering water and whisk lightly until the sugar has dissolved and the mixture is hot to the touch. Take the bowl off the heat and, using an electric mixer, whisk on high speed for 3–5 minutes, or until the mixture holds stiff peaks. Add the vanilla and whisk briefly to combine. Spoon the meringue onto the tarts and spread to cover the lemon curd. Briefly brown the meringue with a blowtorch or under a hot grill (broiler). Serve immediately.

If preparing in advance, store the baked pastry cases in a sealed container for up to 2 days. Add the filling and topping shortly before serving.

Individual Tarte Tatin

MAKES 2

If I were to choose a death row dessert, a classic and perfectly made tarte tatin would definitely be on my shortlist, and would quite possibly be my final choice. The combination of crisp pastry and buttery caramelized apples could only be improved by adding a scoop of vanilla ice cream. These individual tarts would be a wonderful end to a date night dinner, especially when you realize they're not too difficult to make. To keep things simple, I like to use shop-bought puff pastry, but if you have any leftovers of my Flaky Pastry (see page 154), that would also work well.

100g (3½oz) ready-rolled puff pastry

FOR THE FILLING

2 large Granny Smith apples, peeled, cored and quartered

15g (½oz/1 tablespoon) unsalted butter

1 tablespoon lemon juice

FOR THE CARAMEL

50g (1¾oz/¼ cup) caster (superfine or granulated) sugar

A few drops of lemon juice

2 tablespoons water

15g (½oz/1 tablespoon) unsalted butter

Pinch of sea salt flakes

Preheat the oven to 200°C (180°C Fan) 400°F, Gas Mark 6.

Unroll the pastry and use a 10cm (4in) round cookie cutter to stamp out 2 circles. Refrigerate until needed.

To make the filling, slice each apple quarter into 3 lengthways pieces. Place the butter in a small saucepan over a medium heat until just starting to bubble. Add the apples and lemon juice and cook for 2 minutes, stirring gently and frequently. Turn the heat off, place a lid on the pan and set aside for 3 minutes before tipping the apples into a bowl.

To make the caramel, clean the saucepan, then add the sugar, lemon juice and water. Swirl to combine – avoid stirring – and cook over a medium heat until the sugar has dissolved and the syrup has turned a rich amber colour. Don't overcook, because the caramel will cook further as the tarts bake. Turn off the heat, add the butter and salt and stir to combine.

Divide the caramel equally between 2 x 9cm (3½in) ramekins and, being careful not to touch the caramel with your fingers, add the apples, overlapping the slices tightly and neatly. Place the pastry circles on top of the apples and use a round-tipped knife to press the excess pastry down the insides of the ramekins. Pierce a couple of holes in the pastry, then place the dishes on a baking tray (cookie sheet).

Bake for 25 minutes, or until the pastry is golden. Remove from the oven and lightly compress the pastry by sitting a tin of chickpeas (or something similar) on top of each tart. Set aside for 5 minutes to cool slightly.

To serve, run a knife around the inside of the ramekins to loosen the tarts, then carefully invert onto plates. Serve while still hot, with a generous scoop of vanilla ice cream.

Brown Butter Salted Maple Tarts

MAKES 4

These tarts are my take on chess pie, a classic dish from the southern US states. No one really seems to know the origin of the name, but it is thought to have a connection with British baking, and is perhaps related to lemon cheese, an old-fashioned name for lemon curd. The two recipes have a similar composition, and the name (chess/cheese) feels close enough not to be a coincidence. My take on chess pie owes a lot to two renowned US bakeries – Four and Twenty Blackbirds in Brooklyn and Sister Pie in Detroit. The Brooklyn bakery makes a famous chess-style pie with salted honey, and the Detroit bakery makes a similar one using maple syrup.

½ batch Sweet Pastry (see page 152)

Flour, for dusting

1 egg yolk, beaten (optional)

FOR THE FILLING

50g (1¾oz/3½ tablespoons) unsalted butter, diced

60g (2¼oz/¼ cup + 1 teaspoon, packed) light brown sugar

1½ tablespoons cornmeal

¼ teaspoon fine sea salt

½ teaspoon vanilla bean paste

100ml (3½fl oz/⅓ cup + 4 teaspoons) maple syrup (see note below)

50ml (2fl oz/3 tablespoons + 1 teaspoon) double (heavy) cream

30ml (1fl oz/2 tablespoons) dark rum

1 large egg

Sea salt flakes, for sprinkling

NOTE   It's best to use a high-quality dark maple syrup, ideally a Grade B, as it has a strong flavour that will stand up to the other ingredients.

Cut the pastry into 4 equal slices. Lightly flour a work surface and roll each piece of pastry into a circle about 3mm (⅛in) thick. Use to line 4 x 10cm (4in) loose-bottomed tart tins, trimming off any excess. Refrigerate for an hour or so.

Preheat the oven to 200°C (180°C Fan) 400°F, Gas Mark 6.

Line each tart case with a crumpled piece of parchment paper, fill with baking beans or rice and place on a baking tray (cookie sheet). Bake for about 20 minutes, or until the edges are lightly browned, then remove the parchment and beans. Return them to the oven for 5 minutes, until the inside of the pastry is lightly golden. To ensure the pastry remains crisp after filling, you can brush beaten egg yolk inside the tart cases and bake them for a minute or two more to create a barrier that helps prevent a soggy base. Set aside, and lower the oven temperature to 190°C (170°C Fan) 375°F, Gas Mark 5.

To make the filling, place the butter in a small saucepan over a medium heat until it starts to splatter and then foam. Keep heating until it smells warm and nutty and the milk solids have browned, but take care not to let these brown flecks catch and burn. Pour the browned butter into a jug, add the sugar and whisk until it has dissolved. Add the cornmeal, salt, vanilla and maple syrup and whisk to combine. Add the cream, rum and egg and whisk until smooth.

Return the pastry cases to the oven and carefully pour in the maple mixture. Bake for 20–22 minutes, or until slightly puffed with a slight wobble in the centre. Sprinkle with sea salt flakes and set aside until fully cooled.

These tarts are best served on the day they are made, but will keep for up to 2 days if stored in a sealed container.

Matcha Cheesecake Tarts

MAKES 6

These little tarts are inspired by the Hokkaido cheese tarts I became rather enamoured with on my first visit to Japan. The classic version, a barely sweet creamy cheesecake, is the most famous, but it's the matcha version I now make regularly at home. As this recipe uses very small amounts of ingredients for the filling, I often make it to use up leftovers of cream cheese, sour cream and cream I have remaining from other recipes and that aren't enough for anything else.

¼ batch Sweet Pastry (see page 152)

Flour, for dusting

FOR THE FILLING

80g (2¾oz/⅓ cup + 1 teaspoon) cream cheese

3 tablespoons caster (superfine or granulated) sugar

30g (1oz/2 tablespoons) sour cream

40ml (1½fl oz/2 tablespoons + 2 teaspoons) double (heavy) cream, plus an extra splash to go with the egg yolk

2 teaspoons matcha powder

1½ teaspoons cornflour (cornstarch)

½ teaspoon vanilla bean paste

1 large egg, separated

Place all the filling ingredients (except the egg yolk, which you'll use later) in a heatproof bowl set over a pan of simmering water, and heat, stirring constantly with a spatula, until everything is melted and smooth. Continue heating until the mixture has thickened slightly and reached about 75°C (167°F). Take off the heat and, if at all lumpy, pass through a fine mesh sieve into a small bowl. Cover with clingfilm (plastic wrap) and refrigerate until cool.

Cut the pastry into 6 equal slices. Lightly flour a work surface and roll each piece of pastry into a circle about 3mm (⅛in) thick. Using a 9cm (3½in) round cookie cutter, cut each piece into a neat circle. Use the pastry to line a 6-hole muffin tray or 6 mini tart tins roughly the same size as the compartments in a muffin tray. Refrigerate for 30 minutes.

Preheat the oven to 190°C (170°C Fan) 375°F, Gas Mark 5.

Dock the base of each pastry case with a fork, then bake for about 15 minutes, or until golden brown. Set them aside to cool for a few minutes and increase the oven temperature to 230°C (210°C Fan) 450°F, Gas Mark 8.

Spoon or pipe the filling into the pastry cases. Beat the reserved egg yolk with a small splash of cream, then very carefully brush it over the filling. Bake for 5–6 minutes, just until the filling is starting to brown. Set aside to cool completely.

If stored in a sealed container in the refrigerator, these tarts will keep for 2–3 days. The filling will firm up slightly when chilled.

Sour Cherry Galettes

MAKES 4

Sour cherry pie may be a top tier pastry, but a big pie isn't really in the vein of small batch baking. The next best thing, a galette, is still spectacularly good, and significantly easier to put together. Fresh sour cherries have a very short season, so can be hard to source. Thankfully, their frozen counterparts are much easier to come by and are great for spur of the moment crumbles, cobblers and other desserts, such as this one.

½ batch Flaky Pastry (see page 154)

Flour, for dusting

4 tablespoons ground almonds

1 large egg, beaten

Demerara sugar, for sprinkling

FOR THE FILLING

350g (¾lb) frozen sour cherries

75g (2¾oz/¼ cup + 2 tablespoons) caster (superfine or granulated) sugar

1 tablespoon cornflour (cornstarch)

¼ teaspoon almond extract

First make the filling: place the cherries and sugar in a saucepan over a medium heat and cook, stirring occasionally, until the sugar has dissolved and the fruit has released a lot of juice, but hasn't yet broken down. Using a slotted spoon, transfer the fruit to a bowl and set aside. Add the cornflour to the pan and use a mini whisk to combine it with the juice. Bring the liquid to a simmer and cook until it has reduced slightly and is syrupy in texture. Pour this syrup over the fruit, add the almond extract and stir to combine. Refrigerate until fully chilled.

Line a baking tray (cookie sheet) with parchment paper. Cut the pastry into 4 equal slices. Lightly flour a work surface and roll each piece of pastry into a circle about 15–20cm (6–8in) in diameter. Transfer to the prepared tray and refrigerate for 20 minutes.

Preheat the oven to 200ºC (180ºC Fan) 400ºF, Gas Mark 6.

Place a tablespoon of the ground almonds in the middle of each pastry circle and spread evenly, leaving a wide border (roughly 2.5cm/1in) around them. Top with an even layer of the fruit mixture. Fold the edges of the pastry over the fruit, leaving the centre exposed. Brush the pastry with the beaten egg, then sprinkle with some demerara sugar.

Bake for 25–30 minutes, or until the pastry is crisp and golden. Set aside to cool a little before serving hot with a scoop of vanilla ice cream.

Strawberries and Cream Éclairs

MAKES 4

You can't go through the summer in the UK without enjoying strawberries and cream, a traditional summertime treat. Here I've incorporated those flavours into éclairs for a lovely variation on that favourite. Whilst easy to make, like most things, éclairs can best be mastered by repetition, which is no hardship when they're as delicious as this.

1 batch Choux Pastry (see page 156)

Icing (powdered) sugar (optional)

FOR THE FILLING

10 large strawberries

1 tablespoon strawberry jam, shop-bought or homemade (see page 164)

120ml (4fl oz/½ cup) double (heavy) cream

¼ teaspoon vanilla bean paste

Preheat the oven to 190°C (170°C Fan) 375°F, Gas Mark 5. Cut a piece of parchment paper the same size as your baking tray (cookie sheet) and draw 4 x 12cm (5in) lines on the back, spacing them well apart. Place the parchment pencilled-side down on the tray.

Spoon the choux pastry into a piping bag fitted with a French star piping tip. If you find piping tricky, you can chill the dough for an hour or two at this point, making it slightly stiffer and easier to control.

When you're ready, hold the piping bag at roughly a 45-degree angle and pipe along each pencilled line with consistent pressure and movement so that the finished éclair is as straight and even as possible. Use a wet finger to smooth out any pointy or uneven ends.

Before baking, some people like to brush the strips with beaten egg, but I prefer either to lightly spritz them with water and then dust with a little icing sugar, or to mist them with oil (I use an aerosol cake release spray), and in this case I do not dust them with sugar. Both methods help the dough to develop a hollow interior, and also prevent cracking while baking.

Bake for about 30 minutes or until the éclairs are browned and feel crisp to the touch. Turn off the oven and leave them inside to cool for 30 minutes. Remove from the oven and set aside until fully cooled.

To make the filling, select 4 of the strawberries, cut each into 3 slices and set aside. Dice the remaining strawberries, place in a small bowl and mix in the jam.

Place the cream and vanilla in a bowl and whisk until holding very soft peaks. If taken too far at this stage, it will become overwhisked and grainy. Spoon the cream into a piping bag fitted with a plain round piping tip.

Using a serrated knife, cut a lengthways slice off each éclair and set these 'lids' aside. Spoon the diced strawberry mixture into the hollows. Pipe 4 mounds of cream onto each filled éclair, placing a slice of strawberry between each mound. Place the pastry lids on top and dust with a little icing sugar.

Once assembled, the éclairs are best served within a few hours.

NOTE It is possible to pipe and freeze the unbaked dough, ready to bake at a later date from frozen; just add a few more minutes to the baking time. Similarly, the empty baked éclairs can be frozen, but they'll need a short bake to crisp them again before filling.

Feta and Za'atar Bourekas

MAKES 4

These Israeli-inspired bourekas (closely related to the Turkish borek) are filled with feta and za'atar, and are delicious as is. But if you want something extra special, take note of an idea I was introduced to by the baker Uri Scheft: cut the bourekas open and add chopped boiled egg, pickle, tomato and parsley, tahini and zhoug – a feast of flavours and textures in a sort of pastry sandwich.

Flour, for dusting

½ batch Flaky Pastry (see page 154)

2 tablespoons sesame seeds

FOR THE FILLING

100g (3½oz/⅓ cup + 1 tablespoon) cream cheese

50g (1¾oz/¼ cup) crumbled feta cheese

3 teaspoons za'atar

1 large egg, beaten

Preheat the oven to 190ºC (170ºC Fan) 375ºF, Gas Mark 5. Line a baking tray (cookie sheet) with parchment paper.

Lightly flour a work surface and roll the pastry into a square that measures just over 30 x 30cm (12 x 12in). Trim to size, then cut into 4 equal squares.

Place all the filling ingredients in a bowl, reserving a little of the egg for brushing, and mix until evenly combined. Spoon equally into the middle the pastry squares, then brush a little water around each mound. Lift up one corner of the pastry and fold it over the filling to meet the opposite corner, then press the edges together to enclose the filling and form a triangle.

Place the pastries on the prepared tray and brush with the reserved beaten egg. Sprinkle with the sesame seeds and bake for 25–30 minutes, or until the pastry is golden brown. Allow to cool before serving.

If stored in a sealed container, these bourekas will keep for 2 days.

Fennel Sausage Hand Pies

MAKES 6

If I were to make myself lunch for a day of travelling, I can't think of anything I'd rather make than one of these pies. Crisp flaky pastry is generously filled with sausage, fennel, tomato and grated mozzarella. It's the love child of a pizza and a sausage roll.

1 batch Flaky Pastry (see page 154)

Flour, for dusting

200g (7oz/1¾ cups) grated mozzarella cheese

1 large egg, beaten

FOR THE FILLING

1 tablespoon olive oil

1 small onion, diced

1 garlic clove, crushed

1 tablespoon fennel seeds

4 Italian pork sausages, casings removed

185ml (6½fl oz/¾ cup + 1 teaspoon) tomato passata (tomato purée)

Sea salt

First make the filling: heat the oil in a frying pan over low–medium heat. Add the onion, garlic and fennel seeds, season with a little salt, and cook gently until translucent, about 10 minutes. Turn up the heat to medium and add the sausage meat, breaking it up with a wooden spoon. Cook until lightly browned. Pour in the passata and simmer for about 10 minutes, until slightly reduced. Taste and adjust the seasoning as needed, then set aside and cool to room temperature.

Divide the pastry in half. Lightly flour a work surface and roll each piece into a rectangle roughly 35 x 25cm (14 x 10in). Cut each rectangle into 6 smaller rectangles.

Spoon the filling onto half of the pastry pieces, spreading it evenly and leaving a 1cm (½in) clear border around the edge. Top with the cheese. Brush the border around the filling with beaten egg, cover with a second piece of pastry and press the edges together with a fork. Place the pies on a parchment-lined baking tray (cookie sheet) and refrigerate for 1 hour.

Preheat the oven to 200°C (180°C Fan) 400°F, Gas Mark 6.

Brush the chilled pies with the remaining beaten egg, then pierce the top with the tip of a sharp knife. Bake for 35–40 minutes, or until the pastry is golden. Set aside to cool slightly before serving warm or at room temperature.

The baked pies can be stored for up to 3 days in a sealed container, or frozen for up to a month. You can also freeze the unbaked pies and bake them from frozen, adding an extra 5 minutes or so to the baking time.

Chorizo, Manchego and Red Pepper Mini Quiches

MAKES 4

Inspired by the Spanish romesco sauce, these quiches are made with sweet red pepper, sun-dried tomatoes and hazelnuts, with the addition of chorizo and Manchego cheese. I like to serve them topped with a little fresh rocket (arugula) and some extra cheese. Eat them while still warm, or as part of a picnic lunch.

½ batch Flaky Pastry (see page 154)

Flour, for dusting

1 egg yolk, beaten (optional)

FOR THE FILLING

60g (2oz) chorizo, sliced

2 roasted red (bell) peppers from a jar, diced

30g (1oz) sun-dried tomatoes, sliced

1 large egg

100ml (3½fl oz/⅓ cup + 4 teaspoons) double (heavy) cream

Freshly ground black pepper

35g (1¼oz/⅓ cup) grated Manchego cheese

30g (1oz/¼ cup) toasted hazelnuts, roughly chopped

Cut the pastry into 4 equal slices. Lightly flour a work surface and roll each piece of pastry into a circle about 3mm (⅛in) thick. Use to line 4 x 10cm (4in) loose-bottomed tart tins, trimming off any excess. Refrigerate for at least 1 hour.

Preheat the oven to 200ºC (180ºC Fan) 400ºF, Gas Mark 6.

To make the filling, add the chorizo to a frying pan set over a medium heat and cook, turning occasionally, until browned and crisp. Tip into a bowl, then stir in the peppers and tomatoes. Whisk the egg and cream together in a small jug, season with a little black pepper, then stir in the cheese.

Line each tart case with a piece of crumpled parchment paper, fill with baking beans or rice and place on a baking tray (cookie sheet). Bake for about 20 minutes, or until the edges are lightly browned. Remove the parchment and beans, then bake for a further 5 minutes, or until the inside of the pastry is golden. To ensure it remains crisp after filling, you can brush beaten egg yolk inside the tart cases and bake them for a minute or two more to create a barrier that helps prevent a soggy base. Set aside and lower the oven temperature to 190ºC (170ºC Fan) 375ºF, Gas Mark 5.

Spoon the chorizo filling into the pastry cases, then pour over the egg mixture. Finish by sprinkling over the chopped hazelnuts. Bake for 15 minutes, or until the custard is set. Set aside for 15 minutes, before carefully removing the tarts from the tins. Serve while still warm, or allow to cool completely.

If stored in a sealed container in the refrigerator, the quiches will keep for 3–4 days, but the pastry will soften over time. To reheat, place them on a baking tray, cover with foil and bake at 180ºC (160ºC Fan) 350ºF, Gas Mark 4 for about 15 minutes.

COOKIES, BARS AND TREATS

Carrot Cake Sandwich Cookies

MAKES 6

If you're a fan of a traditional carrot cake with plenty of cream cheese frosting, this recipe is for you – a more portable version of the timeless favourite. The cookies have all the classic flavours of the cake, but the texture is a cross between a cookie and a muffin top, perfect for sandwiching together with some cream cheese frosting.

115g (4oz/1 stick) unsalted butter, at room temperature

75g (2¾oz/⅓ cup + 1 teaspoon) caster (superfine or granulated) sugar

75g (2¾oz/⅓ cup) light brown sugar

1 large egg

1 teaspoon vanilla bean paste

175g (6oz/1⅓ cups + 1 tablespoon) plain (all-purpose) flour

½ teaspoon bicarbonate of soda (baking soda)

½ teaspoon baking powder

¼ teaspoon fine sea salt

½ teaspoon ground cinnamon

50g (1¾oz/⅔ cup) rolled oats

50g (1¾oz/heaped ⅓ cup) raisins

85g (3oz/1 cup) grated carrot

FOR THE FROSTING

20g (¾oz/1¾ tablespoons) unsalted butter, at room temperature

35g (1¼oz/⅛ cup + 1 teaspoon) cream cheese, at room temperature

100g (3½oz/¾ cup + 1 tablespoon) icing (powdered) sugar

¼ teaspoon vanilla bean paste

Pinch of fine sea salt

Line 2 baking trays (cookie sheets) with parchment paper.

Using an electric mixer, beat the butter and sugars together in a large bowl until light and fluffy, about 5 minutes. Add the egg and vanilla and beat briefly until fully combined. In a separate bowl, whisk together the flour, bicarbonate of soda, baking powder, salt and cinnamon. Add the oats and raisins and mix briefly to combine. Add this dry mixture to the butter mixture, stirring with a spatula until a dough forms. Add the carrot and mix briefly to distribute.

Using a 60ml (2¼fl oz/¼ cup) mechanical ice-cream scoop or two tablespoons, place 6 scoops of the dough on each prepared tray, spacing them well apart, and refrigerate for 1 hour.

Preheat the oven to 180ºC (160ºC Fan) 350ºF, Gas Mark 4.

Bake the cookies for 17–18 minutes, or until golden brown around the edges and no longer looking wet in the centre. Set aside for 10 minutes, before carefully transferring to a wire rack to cool completely.

To make the frosting, beat the butter and cream cheese together in a bowl until smooth. Add the icing sugar, vanilla and salt and beat until light and fluffy, about 5 minutes. Spoon the frosting onto the base of half the cookies and spread to cover. Sandwich together with the remaining cookies.

If stored in a sealed container, these will keep for 2–3 days.

Chocolate Peanut Butter Cookies

MAKES 6

Hands down, these will be the best peanut butter cookies you ever make – dense and chewy, but also ridiculously easy. They are loosely adapted from the recipe made famous by the Ovenly Bakery in New York. As a further treat, I also dip these in chocolate, because everything is better dipped in chocolate, right?

175g (6oz/¾ cup + 2 teaspoons) light brown sugar

1 large egg

½ teaspoon vanilla extract

Pinch of fine sea salt

225g (8oz/¾ cup + 2 tablespoons) smooth peanut butter, at room temperature

Sea salt flakes, for sprinkling

100g (3½oz) dark chocolate, melted

Place the sugar and egg in a large bowl and whisk together briefly until combined. Add the vanilla and salt and again whisk briefly to combine. Now add the peanut butter and whisk until a thick but smooth dough is formed. Cover the bowl and refrigerate for 30 minutes.

Line a baking tray (cookie sheet) with parchment paper. Using a 60ml (2¼fl oz/¼ cup) mechanical ice-cream scoop or your hands, place 6 scoops or balls of cookie dough on the prepared tray, spacing them well apart. Transfer to the freezer for 10 minutes. Meanwhile, preheat the oven to 180ºC (160ºC Fan) 350ºF, Gas Mark 4.

Sprinkle the chilled cookies with sea salt flakes and bake for 20–22 minutes, or until the cookies have spread a little and the edges are lightly browned. Set aside to cool completely.

To serve, dip the cookies halfway into the melted chocolate and then place back on the lined tray. Refrigerate until the chocolate has set.

If stored in a sealed container, these cookies will keep for 4–5 days.

One Egg Pistachio and Raspberry Meringue Cookies

MAKES 6

If you bake a lot, you constantly need to find a use for leftover egg whites and yolks. This recipe, for cookies flavoured with rose water and coated in chopped pistachios, is one of my favourite ways to use up a solitary egg white. Apart from being quick, it's also adaptable, as you can leave out the raspberry filling and fill the meringues with anything else you like post bake. Why not try sprinkling the meringues with hazelnuts and filling them with hazelnut chocolate spread? Or perhaps a combo of almonds and lemon curd, or cookie crumbs and lime curd?

1 large egg white

Pinch of fine sea salt

Pinch of cream of tartar

65g (2½oz/⅓ cup) caster (superfine or granulated) sugar

1 teaspoon rose water (optional)

40g (1½oz/⅓ cup) chopped pistachios

6 teaspoons raspberry jam, shop-bought or homemade (see page 164)

Preheat the oven to 120ºC (100ºC Fan) 250ºF, Gas Mark ½. Line a baking tray (cookie sheet) with parchment paper.

Place the egg white in a large, spotlessly clean bowl, add the salt and cream of tartar and whisk until foamy. Gradually add the sugar, whisking constantly until the meringue holds stiff peaks. Add the rose water (if using), and whisk briefly to combine. Spoon 6 small mounds of the meringue onto the prepared tray, spacing them well apart, and use a teaspoon to make a well in the middle of each one. Sprinkle with the chopped pistachios, then fill each well with a teaspoon of the jam.

Bake for 1 hour, then turn off the heat and allow the cookies to cool in the oven for another 30–60 minutes. If stored in a sealed container, they will keep for up to a week.

Oatmeal Raisin Cookies

MAKES 4

These cookies are straight-up classics, no twists, no added flavours, because why would you mess with perfection? Like my single cookie recipe (see page 50), this dough is made incredibly quickly, but it needs a little resting in the refrigerator; a couple of hours will do the trick. The finished texture of these cookies is akin to a muffin top: soft and a little chewy.

30g (1oz/2 tablespoons) unsalted butter, melted

70g (2½oz/⅓ cup) light brown sugar

25g (1oz/2 tablespoons) caster (superfine or granulated) sugar

1 large egg

65g (2½oz/scant ½ cup) plain (all-purpose) flour

¼ teaspoon baking powder

¼ teaspoon bicarbonate of soda (baking soda)

¼ teaspoon fine sea salt

60g (2¼oz/¾ cup) rolled oats

65g (2½oz/½ cup) raisins

Place the butter and sugars in a small bowl and whisk together. Add the egg and whisk until the mixture looks smooth and silky.

Combine the flour, baking powder, bicarbonate of soda and salt in a separate bowl, then add to the egg mixture, along with the oats and raisins, stirring with a spatula to form a dough. Refrigerate for 1 hour or so, until slightly firmer.

Preheat the oven to 180ºC (160ºC Fan) 350ºF, Gas Mark 4. Line a baking tray (cookie sheet) with parchment paper.

Using a 60ml (2¼fl oz/¼ cup) mechanical ice-cream scoop or 2 tablespoons, place 4 mounds of dough on the prepared tray, spacing them well apart. Bake for about 12 minutes, or until the edges are golden brown and the centres are a little paler, but not wet. Set aside to cool on the tray for 10 minutes, before transferring to a wire rack to cool completely.

If stored in a sealed container, the cookies will keep for 3–4 days.

NOTE If your raisins seem very dry and firm, it's a good idea to soak them in hot water for 15 minutes before use to prevent them from burning as the cookies bake.

Emergency Chocolate Chip Cookie

MAKES 1

There are times when absolutely nothing but a warm chocolate chip cookie will hit the spot. Bad day at work? Chocolate chip cookie. The end of a great day? Chocolate chip cookie. You never know when the emergency might strike, but thankfully this solitary cookie, made with just a spatula and measuring spoons for true speed and simplicity, is ready for you whenever the need arises, and it will be out of the oven, ready to eat, quicker than you'd ever imagine.

1 tablespoon unsalted butter, melted and slightly cooled

1 tablespoon light brown sugar

1 tablespoon caster (superfine or granulated) sugar

½ tablespoon whole milk

3 tablespoons plain (all-purpose) flour

Pinch of baking powder

Pinch of bicarbonate of soda (baking soda)

Pinch of fine sea salt

2 tablespoons roughly chopped dark chocolate

Preheat the oven to 180°C (160°C Fan) 350°F, Gas Mark 4. Line a baking tray (cookie sheet) with parchment paper.

Place the butter and sugars in a small bowl and mix together using a spatula. Pour in the milk and mix until creamy. Add the flour, baking powder, bicarbonate of soda and salt and mix until a dough forms. Add the chocolate and mix to combine. The dough should be soft but not sticky. If needed, mix in a little extra flour, a teaspoon at a time, adding just enough to make the dough lose its stickiness but not become stiff.

Form the dough into a ball, place on the prepared tray and bake for 16 minutes, or until golden around the edges and a little paler in the centre. Set aside to cool.

The cookie is best eaten on the day it's made.

NOTE Baking uses measuring spoons, not the household spoons you eat your cereal with, so the ingredient should be level with the spoon, not heaped.

Vegan Crinkle Cookies with Tahini and Cardamom

MAKES 4

The combo of chocolate, cardamom and tahini is a match made in heaven. The chocolate is rich and intense, but balanced by the floral cardamom and given a touch of nuttiness by the tahini. As this recipe uses only a small amount of tahini, it's a perfect way of using up that last little scraping in the bottom of the jar.

½ teaspoon ground psyllium husks or ½ tablespoon ground flaxseeds

1½ tablespoons water

50g (1¾oz) dark chocolate, finely chopped

35g (1¼oz/2 tablespoons) tahini

25g (1oz/2 tablespoons) coconut oil

25g (1oz/2 tablespoons) caster (superfine or granulated) sugar

25g (1oz/1 tablespoon + 2 teaspoons) light brown sugar

¼ teaspoon ground cardamom

50g (1¾oz/⅓ cup + 1 tablespoon) plain (all-purpose) flour

10g (¼oz/2 tablespoons) cocoa powder

¼ teaspoon bicarbonate of soda (baking soda)

Pinch of fine sea salt

30g (1oz/¼ cup) icing (powdered) sugar

Place the psyllium husks or flaxseeds in a small bowl, add the water and mix together. Set aside.

Place the chocolate, tahini, coconut oil, sugars and cardamom in a bowl set over a pan of simmering water. Stir occasionally until the chocolate and coconut oil have melted and the mixture is smooth.

In a separate bowl, whisk together the flour, cocoa powder, bicarbonate of soda and salt. Mix the psyllium or flaxseed mixture into the melted chocolate mixture, then pour this mixture into the flour bowl and stir with a spatula to form a dough. Press a sheet of clingfilm (plastic wrap) directly onto the surface of the dough and refrigerate for 4 hours, or until firm.

Preheat the oven to 180ºC (160ºC Fan) 350ºF, Gas Mark 4. Line a baking tray (cookie sheet) with parchment paper.

Divide the chilled dough into 4 equal pieces and roll them into balls. Sift the icing sugar onto a plate and roll the balls in it. Transfer them to the prepared tray, spacing them well apart, and bake for about 15 minutes, or until they have spread and cracked. Set aside and allow to cool fully on the tray before serving.

These are best eaten within 2 days of baking.

Melting Moments

MAKES 6 SANDWICH COOKIES

Possibly my ideal shortbread-style cookies, these are tender and crumbly, with a melt-in-the-mouth texture. They also happen to be a cinch to make by hand, with nothing but a bowl and a spatula. You can fill these cookies with anything you fancy or have lying around or left over from other baking projects. I love them with a little lemon curd, a dollop of dulce de leche, or a little raspberry buttercream.

125g (4½oz/1 stick + 2 teaspoons) unsalted butter, at room temperature

½ teaspoon vanilla bean paste

40g (1½oz/⅓ cup) icing (powdered) sugar

125g (4½oz/1 cup) plain (all-purpose) flour, plus extra for dusting

20g (¾oz/2 tablespoons + 1 teaspoon) cornflour (cornstarch)

Pinch of salt

6 heaped teaspoons jam, curd or buttercream, for the filling

Place the butter in a bowl and beat with a spatula until soft and creamy. Add the vanilla and icing sugar and beat together until smooth. Add the flour, cornflour and salt and mix until a thick, shortbread-like dough forms.

Line a baking tray (cookie sheet) with parchment paper. Using your hands, divide the dough into 12 equal pieces and roll them into balls. Place on the prepared baking tray, spacing them a little apart, and use a fork dipped in flour to flatten them slightly and leave an indent. Refrigerate for 20 minutes, or until the dough is firm. Meanwhile, preheat the oven to 180°C (160°C Fan) 350°F, Gas Mark 4.

Bake the cookies for about 15 minutes, or until pale golden brown around the edges and a touch paler on top. Set aside until completely cooled.

Spread the underside of half the cookies with your filling of choice and sandwich together with the remaining cookies.

If stored in a sealed container, these cookies will keep for about 3 days.

Lime Coconut Macaroons

MAKES 4

These little macaroons are a perfect excuse for using up that bag of desiccated coconut languishing at the back of your kitchen cupboard. I have given these a twist by adding lime zest, which gives them the vibe of a Key lime pie. To make them even more special, they are dipped and drizzled with chocolate.

50g (1¾oz/¼ cup) caster (superfine or granulated) sugar

Zest of 1 lime

1 large egg white

Pinch of fine sea salt

½ teaspoon vanilla bean paste

80g (2¾oz/1 cup) desiccated coconut

2 teaspoons golden syrup

50g (1¾oz) dark or milk chocolate, for decoration

Preheat the oven to 180ºC (160ºC Fan) 350ºF, Gas Mark 4. Line a baking tray (cookie sheet) with parchment paper.

Place the sugar and lime zest in a small bowl and rub together with your fingertips to help to release the lime oil and intensify its flavour in the finished macaroons.

Place the egg white and salt in a large bowl and whisk together until foamy. Add the lime sugar and vanilla paste and whisk briefly until the mixture resembles shaving foam. Using a spatula, stir in the coconut and golden syrup until well combined.

Divide the macaroon mixture into 4 equal pieces and roll them into balls. Place on the prepared baking tray, spacing them a little apart, and bake for 15–18 minutes, or until starting to brown. Set aside until completely cooled.

Place the chocolate in a heatproof bowl over a pan of simmering water, making sure the base of the bowl is not touching the water, and leave to melt. Allow to cool a little, then dip the base of each macaroon in it and return to the parchment-lined tray. Using a spoon or piping bag, drizzle the remaining chocolate over the top of the macaroons.

If stored in a sealed container, these will keep for 3–4 days.

Snickerdoodle Cheesecake Bars

MAKES 4–6

Tender cookies rolled in cinnamon sugar, Snickerdoodles are comforting and far too simple to be as good as they are. This recipe takes the basic idea of that simple soft cookie and marries it with cream cheese, so it's like a cheesecake gussied up for a fancy night out. Once baked, the outside of the cookie is nice and crisp, and where it meets the cheesecake, a little gooey. It's a dreamy combination of textures and tastes.

60g (2¼oz/4 tablespoons) unsalted butter, plus extra for greasing

115g (4oz/½ cup + 1 teaspoon, packed) light brown sugar

2 large egg yolks

100g (3½oz/¾ cup + 1 tablespoon) plain (all-purpose) flour

¼ teaspoon bicarbonate of soda (baking soda)

Large pinch of fine sea salt

½ teaspoon ground cinnamon

FOR THE FILLING

150g (5½oz/⅔ cup) cream cheese, at room temperature

50g (1¾oz/¼ cup) caster (superfine or granulated) sugar

½ tablespoon cornflour (cornstarch)

½ teaspoon vanilla bean paste

1 large egg white

FOR THE TOPPING

1 tablespoon caster (superfine or granulated) sugar

½ teaspoon ground cinnamon

Preheat the oven to 180°C (160°C Fan) 350°F, Gas Mark 4. Lightly grease a 23 x 13cm (9 x 5in) loaf tin, and line it with a strip of parchment paper that overhangs the long sides, securing it in place with metal binder clips.

Place the butter and sugar in a bowl and beat together for 2–3 minutes, until evenly combined. Add the egg yolks and beat until light and fluffy, about 2 minutes more. Add the remaining dry ingredients and mix together until a smooth dough forms.

Scrape half the dough into the prepared loaf tin and press into an even layer. If it is too sticky to spread easily, using lightly wet hands will help. Bake for about 25 minutes, until lightly browned. Set aside to cool.

Meanwhile, place all the filling ingredients in a small bowl and beat until smooth and evenly combined. Spread the filling evenly over the dough in the tin. Break the remaining dough into small pieces, press them flat between your fingers and arrange over the surface to cover the filling completely.

Combine the caster sugar and cinnamon in a small bowl, then sprinkle about half of this mixture on top. Bake for about 30 minutes, until the topping feels crisp.

Remove from the oven and sprinkle with the remaining sugar. Set aside for 1 hour before transferring to the refrigerator to cool completely. Cut into slices to serve.

If stored in a sealed container in the refrigerator, these bars will keep for 2–3 days. They can also be frozen for up to a month.

Biscoff-Stuffed Brownies

MAKES 4

I cannot keep jars of Biscoff spread in the house – they present a very real danger. If the jar is open, or, let's be honest, even if it's not, a spoon will magically appear in my hand, willing me to take a bite. So when I do have some in the house and I want to use it in something rather than letting it tempt me late at night, these brownies are my favourite way to bake with it. I get a treat and can share the rest or freeze them for a later date.

50g (1¾oz/3½ tablespoons) unsalted butter, diced, plus extra for greasing

50g (1¾oz/⅓ cup + 1 tablespoon) plain (all-purpose) flour

15g (½oz/3 tablespoons) cocoa powder

Pinch of fine sea salt

70g (2½oz) dark chocolate (65–75% cocoa solids)

50g (1¾oz/¼ cup) caster (superfine or granulated) sugar

50g (1¾oz/3 tablespoons + 1 teaspoon, packed) light brown sugar

1 large egg

1 teaspoon vanilla extract

75g (2¾oz/⅓ cup) Biscoff spread

Preheat the oven to 180°C (160°C Fan) 350°F, Gas Mark 4. Lightly grease a 23 x 13cm (9 x 5in) loaf tin, and line it with a strip of parchment paper that overhangs the long sides, securing it in place with metal binder clips.

Sift the flour, cocoa powder and salt into a large bowl and whisk to combine.

Place the butter and chocolate in a bowl set over a pan of simmering water, stirring occasionally until fully melted. Set aside.

In another bowl, whisk together the sugars, egg and vanilla until light and fluffy. Pour in the melted chocolate and whisk until smooth and fully combined. Add the contents of the flour bowl and fold together.

Scrape half the batter into the prepared tin and spread evenly. Spoon or pipe the Biscoff spread over the batter, gently smoothing it evenly and leaving a clear narrow border around the edge. This is easier to do if you warm the spread ever so slightly before use. Add the remaining brownie batter, gently smoothing it over the Biscoff layer to avoid disturbing it too much.

Bake for 22 minutes, until the brownie mixture is slightly puffed. Set aside to cool for 30 minutes, before transferring to the refrigerator for a few hours until thoroughly chilled. This chilling makes it easier to slice the brownies, but also helps to give a dense fudgy texture.

If stored in a sealed container, the brownies will keep for up to 4 days. They can also be frozen for 2 months.

Coffee and Caramelized White Chocolate Meringues

MAKES 4

Meringues are a great way to use up leftover egg whites, but a plain meringue can sometimes be a little underwhelming. Here I've given the classic mixture a little makeover, swirling it with instant espresso powder and chunks of deliciously caramelized white chocolate to give a fantastic bittersweet flavour. This recipe is inspired by a caramelized white chocolate meringue served at the wonderful Ty Melin bakery in Cardiff.

2 large egg whites

Pinch of fine sea salt

Pinch of cream of tartar

160g (5¾oz/¾ cup + 2 teaspoons) caster (superfine or granulated) sugar

1 teaspoon instant espresso powder, plus extra for sprinkling

70g (2½oz) caramelized white chocolate, roughly chopped

Preheat the oven to 110°C (90°C Fan) 225°F, Gas Mark ¼. Line a baking tray (cookie sheet) with parchment paper.

Place the egg whites in a bowl and whisk in the salt and cream of tartar until the mixture looks a little like shaving foam. Slowly rain in the sugar a spoonful at a time, whisking constantly until the meringue holds stiff peaks. Sprinkle in the coffee and chocolate and fold together briefly, just a couple times, to swirl them through the meringue mixture.

Spoon 4 equal mounds of the mixture onto the prepared tray, spacing them well apart, and sprinkle with a little extra coffee powder. Bake for 1½–2 hours, or until dry and crisp, and they can be lifted easily from the parchment. If you bake on the shorter end of the timescale, the finished meringues will have a softer centre than if you bake for longer. Turn the oven off but leave the meringues inside for an hour to cool down slowly.

If stored in a sealed container in a cool, dry place, the meringues will keep for at least a week.

CAKES

Bakery-Style Blueberry Muffins

MAKES 4

These muffins are the result of challenging myself to see just how many blueberries I could pack into one muffin without it falling apart. Being bakery-style, they are big and generous, packed full of fruit and have a great crunch from the generous streusel topping. If you want to make the muffins even simpler, you can skip the streusel and sprinkle with demerara sugar instead.

35g (1¼oz/2½ tablespoons) unsalted butter, diced

50g (1¾oz/¼ cup) caster (superfine or granulated) sugar

Zest of ¼ lemon (optional)

80g (2¾oz/⅓ cup) sour cream or buttermilk or yogurt

1 large egg white

85g (3oz/⅔ cup) plain (all-purpose) flour

1 teaspoon baking powder

¼ teaspoon fine sea salt

170g (6oz) blueberries

FOR THE STREUSEL TOPPING

60g (2¼oz/scant ½ cup) plain (all-purpose) flour

35g (1¼oz/3 tablespoons) caster (superfine or granulated) sugar

40g (1½oz/3 tablespoons) unsalted butter, melted

Preheat the oven to 180ºC (160ºC Fan) 350ºF, Gas Mark 4. Place four paper cases (liners) in a muffin tray.

First make the streusel: place the flour and sugar in a small bowl and drizzle over the melted butter, stirring with a knife until the mixture clumps together. Use your hands to form it into a ball of dough, then refrigerate until needed.

To make the muffins, melt the butter, then pour into a mixing bowl. Add the sugar, lemon zest (if using), sour cream and egg white and mix until smooth. In a separate bowl, whisk together the flour, baking powder and salt. Add the butter mixture along with the blueberries and stir gently and briefly, just until a thick batter forms. Don't worry about it being perfectly smooth; it's important not to overmix, as it can easily become tough.

Divide the batter evenly between the paper cases. Crumble the chilled streusel over the top and bake for about 25 minutes, or until golden brown and a skewer inserted into the muffins comes out clean. Set aside to cool in the tray for 10 minutes, before carefully transferring to a wire rack to cool completely.

TIP The batter can overspill the cases while baking, so to prevent the muffins sticking to the tray, I brush the top of it with a little oil before lining with the paper cases.

Black-Bottom Muffins

MAKES 4–6

Black-bottom cakes are simply chocolate cakes topped with a cheesecake mixture. The topping can be added in the form of a cream cheese frosting, but normally the cheesecake is baked onto the cake itself. There is lots of choice when it comes to the liquid used in the cake batter, Guinness or buttermilk being classic, but anything with a tang would work well; I've even used root beer with great success.

70g (2½oz/5 tablespoons) unsalted butter, plus extra for greasing

75ml (2¾fl oz/¼ cup + 1 tablespoon) Guinness, root beer or buttermilk

20g (¾oz/¼ cup) cocoa powder

100g (3½oz/⅓ cup + 2 tablespoons) light brown sugar

100g (3½oz/⅔ cup + 2 tablespoons) plain (all-purpose) flour

¼ teaspoon bicarbonate of soda (baking soda)

¼ teaspoon fine sea salt

1 large egg white

50g (1¾oz/¼ cup) milk chocolate chips

FOR THE CHEESECAKE TOPPING

60g (2¼oz/¼ cup) cream cheese, at room temperature

1 large egg yolk

1 tablespoon caster (superfine or granulated) sugar

½ teaspoon vanilla bean paste

Preheat the oven to 180ºC (160ºC Fan) 350ºF, Gas Mark 4. Lightly grease a 6-hole muffin tray. Start by placing all the topping ingredients in a small bowl and stirring until smooth. Refrigerate until needed.

To make the cake, place the butter, Guinness, cocoa powder and sugar in a small saucepan over a low–medium heat and stir constantly until the butter has melted and the mixture is smooth. Set aside to cool for a few minutes.

Place the flour, bicarbonate of soda and salt in a bowl and stir to combine. Once the butter mixture is just warm, whisk in the egg white, then pour the mixture into the flour and stir to form a smooth batter. Spoon into the prepared muffin tray. Add small dollops of the chilled topping, then use a skewer to swirl them gently into the batter. Sprinkle with the chocolate chips and bake for 13–15 minutes, or until the cakes spring back to a light touch.

Remove the muffins from the tray and set aside to cool. These are best eaten within 2 days of baking.

NOTE   This recipe makes 6 little cakes, but if you want them more substantial, bake the batter in 4 large tulip muffin cases. They will take 17–18 minutes.

Sweet and Salty Chocolate Cake

MAKES 6 SERVINGS

Here's a fabulous little chocolate cake, perfectly moist and fudgy, layered with a sweet and salty dulce de leche buttercream. This is the definition of easy and, for me, the ideal cake for a celebration.

45g (1½oz/3 tablespoons) unsalted butter, diced, plus extra for greasing

50g (1¾oz) dark chocolate (65–70% cocoa solids)

80g (2¾oz/½ cup + 2 tablespoons) plain (all-purpose) flour

50g (1¾oz/½ cup) wholemeal (wholewheat) or white rye flour

½ teaspoon baking powder

1 teaspoon bicarbonate of soda (baking soda)

¼ teaspoon fine sea salt

125g (4½oz/½ cup + 1 tablespoon) light brown sugar

25g (1oz/⅓ cup) cocoa powder

100ml (3½fl oz/⅓ cup + 4 teaspoons) hot black coffee

100ml (3½fl oz/⅓ cup + 4 teaspoons) buttermilk

1 large egg

FOR THE BUTTERCREAM

75g (2¾oz/⅓ cup) unsalted butter, at room temperature

75g (2¾oz/½ cup + 2 tablespoons) icing (powdered) sugar

100g (3½oz/⅓ cup) dulce de leche

¼ teaspoon sea salt

Preheat the oven to 180°C (160°C Fan) 350°F, Gas Mark 4. Lightly grease 2 x 15cm (6in) round cake tins and line the bases with parchment paper.

Place the butter and chocolate in a heatproof bowl set over a pan of simmering water and heat, stirring occasionally, until the ingredients are fully melted. Alternatively, melt in a microwave, using short bursts of heat to prevent the mixture from burning. Set aside.

Place the flours in a large bowl, add the baking powder, bicarbonate of soda, salt, brown sugar and cocoa powder and whisk together to combine. If any lumps remain, press the mixture through a fine mesh sieve using the back of a spoon. Make a well in the middle of these dry ingredients and set aside.

Pour the coffee and buttermilk into the chocolate mixture and whisk to combine. Add the egg and whisk again. Pour this mixture into the flour bowl and whisk briefly, just until the batter is smooth. Divide the batter between the prepared tins and spread evenly. Bake for 20–25 minutes, or until the cakes spring back to a light touch and are starting to come away from the sides of the tins. Set aside for 15 minutes, before carefully inverting the cakes onto a wire rack to cool completely.

To make the buttercream, place the butter and icing sugar in a bowl and beat for about 5 minutes, or until light and fluffy. Add the dulce de leche and beat for 2 minutes, until fully combined. Add the salt and beat briefly.

Spread half the buttercream over what will be the base layer of the cake. Top with the second cake, then spread the remaining buttercream over the surface.

If stored in a sealed container, this cake will keep for 3–4 days.

Peach Sour Cream Crumb Cake

MAKES 6 SERVINGS

In the UK, peaches seem to be nigh on impossible to get at the perfect stage of ripeness – they're either rock hard or mushy, especially if bought from supermarkets. Thankfully, peaches on the firm side have lots of uses, from jam to all sorts of bakes, and the cooking even helps to intensify the flavour. This simple cake, a twist on the classic crumb cake, is dense and tender, studded with fragrant peaches and finished with a crisp crumb topping. It makes a lovely teatime treat, but can also be dressed up as a dessert with cream or crème fraîche. If you happen to have any leftover crumble topping from the recipe on page 101, you can substitute it for the one below.

50g (1¾oz/3½ tablespoons) unsalted butter, at room temperature, plus extra for greasing

75g (2¾oz/¼ cup + 2 tablespoons) caster (superfine or granulated) sugar

1 large egg

1 teaspoon vanilla extract

80g (2¾oz/⅔ cup) plain (all-purpose) flour

50g (1¾oz/½ cup) ground almonds

¾ teaspoon baking powder

¼ teaspoon fine sea salt

65g (2½oz/¼ cup + 1 teaspoon) sour cream

1 large firm but ripe peach, diced

FOR THE CRUMB TOPPING

75g (2¾oz/½ cup + 2 tablespoons) plain (all-purpose) flour

50g (1¾oz/¼ cup) caster (superfine or granulated) sugar

Pinch of fine sea salt

65g (2½oz/4½ tablespoons) unsalted butter, diced and chilled

First make the topping: combine the flour, sugar and salt in a bowl. Add the butter and toss to coat before rubbing in with your fingertips to form a crumble mixture. Bring together into a ball of dough and refrigerate until needed.

Preheat the oven to 180°C (160°C Fan) 350°F, Gas Mark 4. Lightly grease a 15cm (6in) round cake tin and line the base with parchment paper.

To make the cake, place the butter and sugar in a large bowl and use an electric mixer to beat together until light and fluffy, about 5 minutes. Add the egg and vanilla and beat briefly to combine. In a separate bowl mix together the flour, almonds, baking powder and salt. Add this to the butter mixture and beat briefly to combine. Add the sour cream and mix to form a smooth cake batter. Scrape it into the prepared tin and spread evenly. Sprinkle the diced peach over the surface, then add the topping by crumbling it with your fingers.

Bake for about 50 minutes, or until a skewer inserted into the centre of the cake comes out clean. Set aside to cool for 15 minutes, before carefully turning onto a wire rack to cool completely.

If stored in a sealed container, this cake will keep for 2–3 days.

Japanese Jiggly Cheesecake with Passion Fruit Butterscotch Sauce

MAKES 6 SERVINGS

Japanese cheesecake is the lightest and fluffiest version of cheesecake I've ever come across. In fact, when I was in Osaka I wanted to try it so much that it being available only as a whole cake didn't put me off. We bought the whole thing and ate it in our hotel room. I wouldn't want to admit how much we got through in one sitting. The method of making it reminds me of a chiffon cake, and the texture isn't far off either. I like to accompany it with a passion fruit butterscotch sauce, one of my all-time favourites.

30g (1oz/2 tablespoons) unsalted butter, plus extra for greasing

125g (4½oz/½ cup + 1 tablespoon) cream cheese, at room temperature

85ml (3fl oz/⅓ cup + 1 teaspoon) whole milk

1 teaspoon vanilla bean paste

Zest of ½ lemon

1 tablespoon lemon juice

20g (¾oz/2 tablespoons + 1 teaspoon) plain (all-purpose) flour

1 tablespoon cornflour (cornstarch)

¼ teaspoon fine sea salt

3 large eggs, separated

Pinch of cream of tartar

75g (2¾oz/¼ cup + 2 tablespoons) caster (superfine or granulated) sugar

FOR THE SAUCE

150g (5½oz/⅔ cup packed) light brown sugar

100g (3½oz/7 tablespoons) unsalted butter

150ml (5fl oz/½ cup + 2 tablespoons) double (heavy) cream

50g (1¾oz/4 tablespoons) passion fruit pulp

This is best baked in the oven with the fan turned off to prevent the cake from cracking, so preheat to 200°C (400°F), Gas Mark 6. Lightly grease a deep 15cm (6in) round cake tin, lining the base and sides with parchment paper that extends 2cm (¾in) above the rim.

Place the butter, cream cheese, milk and vanilla in a bowl set over a pan of simmering water and heat, stirring occasionally, until melted and smooth. Set aside until cool, then add the lemon zest and juice, whisking to combine. Sift the flour, cornflour and salt over the cream cheese mixture and whisk until smooth. Add the egg yolks and whisk briefly to combine.

In a clean bowl, whisk the egg whites and cream of tartar until foamy. Add the sugar a little at a time, whisking constantly, until the meringue holds glossy soft peaks. Add a third of the meringue to the batter and use a balloon whisk to fold together. Add the remaining egg whites a third at a time, folding gently until evenly mixed. Pour the batter into the prepared tin and tap firmly on the work surface a few times to knock out any large air pockets. Place a large roasting tray in the oven and sit the cake in it. Pour enough hot water into the tray to come 2.5cm (1in) up the side of the cake tin.

Bake for about 15 minutes, then lower the temperature to 140°C (275°F) Gas Mark 1 and open the oven for 5–10 seconds to release the steam. Bake for another 45 minutes, or until the cake is lightly browned and springs back to a light touch, and a skewer inserted into the middle comes out clean. Lift the cake out of the water and set aside to cool for 15 minutes, before carefully transferring it to a serving plate. I like to serve the cake at room temperature, but if you're making it ahead, you can refrigerate it for up to 3 days, although the texture will become a little firmer.

To make the sauce, place the sugar and butter in a small saucepan over a medium heat, stirring occasionally, until the butter is melted and the mixture is bubbling. Continue heating for 2–3 minutes, stirring regularly, before adding the cream. Cook at a gentle simmer for about 5 minutes. Remove from the heat and stir in the passion fruit pulp. Pour into a jug and set aside until needed.

Serve slices of the cake with plenty of the passion fruit sauce.

Brown Butter Miso Banana Bread

MAKES 4–6 SERVINGS

This recipe might sound like a hipster's shopping list (does that make me a hipster?) but a banana bread made with both browned butter and white miso is very special. The browned butter adds a rich, warming nuttiness, while the miso lends a gentle savoury note and has the effect of deepening all the other flavours in the cake.

75g (2¾oz/⅔ stick) unsalted butter, diced, plus extra for greasing

115g (4oz/⅔ cup + 4 tablespoons) plain (all-purpose) flour

¾ teaspoon baking powder

¼ teaspoon fine sea salt

100g (3½oz) very ripe banana (about 1 large banana)

50ml (2fl oz/3 tablespoons + 1 teaspoon) sour cream

75g (2¾oz/⅓ cup) light brown sugar

1 large egg

¼ teaspoon vanilla bean paste

2 tablespoons white miso paste

Demerara sugar, for sprinkling

Preheat the oven to 180°C (160°C Fan) 350°F, Gas Mark 4. Lightly grease a 23 x 13cm (9 x 5in) loaf tin and line it with a strip of parchment paper that overhangs the long sides, securing it in place with metal binder clips.

Place the flour, baking powder and salt in a bowl and whisk to combine. In a separate bowl, mash the banana to a rough paste, then add the sour cream, sugar, egg, vanilla and miso and stir together until fully combined.

Place the diced butter in a small saucepan over a medium heat until it starts to splatter and then foam. Keep heating until it smells warm and nutty and the milk solids have browned, but take care not to let these brown flecks catch and burn. Pour the browned butter into the banana mixture and whisk to combine. Add the flour mixture and mix briefly, just until a smooth batter forms.

Scrape the batter into the prepared tin and spread evenly. Sprinkle liberally with demerara sugar, then bake for 35–40 minutes, or until the cake springs back to a light touch. Set aside for 10 minutes, before lifting out onto a wire rack to cool completely. Cut into thick slices to serve.

If stored in a sealed container, the cake will keep for at least 4 days.

Cinnamon Bun Slices

MAKES 6 SERVINGS

Made with melted butter so that the batter comes together in a flash, this is the cake you whip up when guests unexpectedly announce their imminent arrival. The joy in this cake, beyond the ease with which it is made (no bread dough required), is the cinnamon butter that you swirl into the batter, creating little pockets of spiced goodness in every slice.

50g (1¾oz/3½ tablespoons) unsalted butter, diced, plus extra for greasing

100g (3½oz/½ cup) caster (superfine or granulated) sugar

1 large egg

65ml (2½fl oz/¼ cup + 1 teaspoon) double (heavy) cream

¼ teaspoon vanilla bean paste

100g (3½oz/¾ cup + 1 tablespoon) plain (all-purpose) flour

¾ teaspoon baking powder

Pinch of fine sea salt

FOR THE CINNAMON BUTTER

25g (1oz/1¾ tablespoons) unsalted butter, at room temperature

25g (1oz/2 tablespoons) light brown sugar

2 teaspoons ground cinnamon

Small pinch of fine sea salt

FOR THE GLAZE

50g (1¾oz/⅓ cup + 1 tablespoon) icing (powdered) sugar, sifted

1 tablespoon whole milk

¼ teaspoon vanilla bean paste

Preheat the oven to 180° (160°C Fan) 350°F, Gas Mark 4. Lightly grease a 23 x 13cm (9 x 5in) loaf tin and line with a strip of parchment paper that overhangs the long sides, securing it in place with metal binder clips.

First make the cinnamon butter: place all the ingredients for it in a bowl and beat together until a very soft paste forms. Set aside.

To make the cake, melt the diced butter in a small pan over a medium heat, then set aside. Place the sugar, egg, cream and vanilla in a bowl and whisk together until smooth and combined. Add the flour, baking powder and salt and whisk again, just until a smooth batter forms. Pour in the melted butter and stir gently with the whisk, just until fully combined. Scrape the batter into the prepared tin and spread evenly.

Spoon little dollops of the cinnamon butter over the batter, then use a skewer or chopstick to gently swirl them in. Bake for about 25 minutes, or until the cake springs back to a light touch and is just starting to come away from the sides of the tin. Turn off the oven and set the cake aside for 15 minutes, before carefully transferring to a wire rack to cool completely.

When the cake is cold, reheat the oven to 180° (160°C Fan) 350°F, Gas Mark 4. Combine the glaze ingredients in a bowl and mix together until smooth and pourable. Drizzle the glaze all over the cake, then return it to the oven for a couple of minutes, or until the glaze is set.

Serve thin slices of the cake alongside big mugs of coffee. Once sliced, it is best eaten that day, but the slices can also be frozen for up to a month.

Sticky Prune Teacakes

MAKES 6

While these little cakes look unassuming, their taste belies their appearance. With the flavours of prunes, black tea, molasses and rye flour, they are the best combination of sticky toffee pudding, teacake and gingerbread. The inspiration came from one of my favourite London coffee shops, Esters in Stoke Newington, which occasionally makes something similar, and whose version has been stuck in my head ever since trying it.

40g (1½oz/3 tablespoons) unsalted butter, plus extra for greasing

115g (4oz) ready-to-eat prunes, halved

150ml (5fl oz/½ cup + 2 tablespoons) black tea (I like to use Earl Grey)

75g (2¾oz/⅓ cup) light brown sugar

1 tablespoon black treacle (molasses)

1 large egg

75g (2¾oz/¾ cup) wholemeal (wholewheat) rye flour

25g (1oz/3 tablespoons) plain (all-purpose) flour

¼ teaspoon fine sea salt

1 teaspoon baking powder

½ teaspoon bicarbonate of soda (baking soda)

Demerara sugar, for sprinkling

Preheat the oven to 180°C (160°C Fan) 350°F, Gas Mark 4. Lightly grease a 6-hole muffin tray.

Place the prunes in a small saucepan, pour in the tea and bring to a simmer over a medium heat. Continue simmering, stirring occasionally, until almost all the liquid has been absorbed.

Meanwhile, place the butter, sugar and treacle in a bowl and beat together until light and fluffy, about 5 minutes. Add the egg and beat until fully combined. In another bowl, whisk together the flours, salt and baking powder. Add to the butter mixture and mix briefly, just to combine.

Take the pan of prunes off the heat, add the bicarbonate of soda and stir together just until it starts to foam. Add to the batter and mix briefly until fully combined.

Spoon the batter into the prepared muffin tray and sprinkle liberally with demerara sugar. Bake for about 20 minutes, or until the cakes spring back to a light touch. Allow to cool for 5 minutes, before carefully transferring to a wire rack to cool completely.

If stored in a sealed container, these cakes will keep for at least 4 days.

Old-Fashioned Cake Doughnuts

MAKES 4

I know what you're thinking, but before you completely dismiss the idea of cake doughnuts, hear me out. Sure, a yeasted doughnut has its place, but a well-made cake doughnut is a thing of beauty – moist, tender and also incredibly easy to make. Like a regular doughnut, it needs to be fried; the difference lies in the dough, which is made with buttermilk and a hint of nutmeg, and refrigerated for a couple of hours before being rolled out and cut into circles. The doughnuts are finished with a simple vanilla glaze, and taste great alongside a steaming mug of coffee.

125g (4½oz/1 cup) plain (all-purpose) flour, plus extra for dusting

¾ teaspoon baking powder

¼ teaspoon bicarbonate of soda (baking soda)

¼ teaspoon fine sea salt

⅛ teaspoon ground nutmeg

50g (1¾oz/¼ cup) caster (superfine or granulated) sugar

15g (½oz/1 tablespoon) unsalted butter, melted and cooled

2 large egg yolks

1 teaspoon vanilla bean paste

60ml (2¼fl oz/¼ cup) buttermilk

Vegetable oil, for deep-frying

FOR THE GLAZE

150g (5½oz/1¼ cups) icing (powdered) sugar, sifted

½ teaspoon vanilla bean paste

30ml (1fl oz/2 tablespoons) whole milk

Pinch of fine sea salt

Place the flour in a large bowl, add the baking powder, bicarbonate of soda, salt, nutmeg and sugar and whisk together to combine. Make a well in the centre, add the butter, egg yolks, vanilla and buttermilk and mix with a spatula until a smooth dough forms. The mixture should be soft and tacky, but not over sticky. Cover the bowl and refrigerate for 1–2 hours, or until the dough has firmed up a little, making it easier to handle.

Lightly flour a work surface and roll out the dough to a thickness of 5–8mm (¼–⅜in). Using a 9cm (3½in) round cookie cutter, stamp out as many circles as you can. On the first roll you'll likely only get 2, but by gently pressing the scraps together, you'll be able to re-roll and cut out 2 more. Place the circles on a parchment-lined baking tray (cookie sheet) and use a 3cm (1¼in) round cookie cutter to cut a hole in the middle of each doughnut. Place the stamped-out holes on the tray alongside the rings and place the tray in the refrigerator.

Meanwhile, pour enough oil into a small saucepan to come about two-thirds of the way up the inside. Place over a medium heat and bring to 160–170°C/320–338°F. If you don't have a thermometer, drop a small cube of bread into the oil and if it browns in 15 seconds, the oil is ready for frying. At that point, turn the heat down a little, carefully place one doughnut at a time in the oil and fry for 2 minutes, flipping just once at the halfway point. When golden brown, use a slotted spoon to transfer the doughnut to a tray lined with kitchen paper (paper towel) to drain. Repeat this step to make 3 more doughnuts.

Combine the glaze ingredients in a bowl and mix to form a thin, pourable liquid. Dip the doughnuts into the glaze, ensuring they are coated all over. Place on a wire rack and leave until set, about 20–30 minutes.

These doughnuts are best eaten on the day they are made.

Pistachio, Raspberry and Rose Snack Cake

MAKES 6 SERVINGS

This is the perfect cake to enjoy with a cup of tea, something citrusy, like an Earl Grey. The cake itself isn't too sweet, so I sometimes like to add a simple glaze made with lemon and rose water to give it a sweet floral finish. However, the cake is moist from the pistachios, so you can omit the glaze if you prefer.

115g (4oz/1 stick) unsalted butter, at room temperature, plus extra for greasing

100g (3½oz/½ cup) caster (superfine or granulated) sugar

Zest of 1 lemon

2 large eggs

70g (2½oz/½ cup + 1 tablespoon) plain (all-purpose) flour

1 teaspoon baking powder

¼ teaspoon fine sea salt

100g (3½oz/¾ cup) pistachios, coarsely ground, plus 2 tablespoons slivered or chopped pistachios

100g (3½oz) raspberries

Edible rose petals

FOR THE GLAZE (OPTIONAL)

Juice of ½ lemon

2 teaspoons rose water

150g (5½oz/1¼ cups) icing (powdered) sugar, sifted

½ teaspoon vanilla bean paste

Preheat the oven to 180ºC (160ºC Fan) 350ºF, Gas Mark 4. Lightly grease a 15cm (6in) cake tin and line the base with parchment paper.

Place the butter, sugar and lemon zest in a bowl and beat together until light and fluffy, about 5 minutes. Beat in the eggs one at a time, ensuring the first is fully combined before adding the second. Place the flour in a separate bowl and mix in the baking powder, salt and ground pistachios. Add to the butter mixture and stir together gently until a smooth batter forms.

Briefly fold two-thirds of the raspberries through the batter, then scrape into the prepared tin and spread evenly. If making the cake *without* a glaze, scatter the remaining raspberries and the chopped pistachios on top now. If making a glaze, set the remaining berries and the nuts aside for later.

Bake for about 50 minutes, or until the cake is golden and springs back to a light touch. Set aside to cool in the tin for 15–20 minutes, before inverting it onto a wire rack to cool completely.

If making the glaze, combine all the ingredients for it in a bowl and mix to form a thick but free-flowing liquid. Pour onto the cake, spreading it over the surface and using a spoon to tease it into dripping down the sides. Scatter over the reserved berries, the pistachios and rose petals.

If not using the glaze, I still like to scatter the cake with some rose petals for decoration.

If stored in a sealed container, this cake will keep for 4–5 days.

Raspberry and Lemon Mini Bundt Cakes

MAKES 4

Perfect for afternoon tea, these adorable little cakes are quick to whip up, as they're made with olive oil. They're also incredibly pretty, thanks to a vibrant glaze made with puréed raspberries and a decoration of dried cornflowers.

75ml (2¾fl oz/⅓ cup) olive oil, plus extra for greasing

100g (3½oz/¾ cup + 1 tablespoon) plain (all-purpose) flour, plus extra for dusting

85g (3oz/¼ cup + 3 tablespoons) caster (superfine or granulated) sugar

Zest of 1 lemon

1 teaspoon vanilla extract

1 large egg white

85ml (3fl oz/⅓ cup + 1 teaspoon) sour cream

1 teaspoon baking powder

¼ teaspoon fine sea salt

70g (2½oz) raspberries, halved, plus a few extra for decoration

Dried cornflowers, for decoration

FOR THE GLAZE

50g (1¾oz) raspberries

1 tablespoon caster (superfine or granulated) sugar

120g (4¼oz/1 cup) icing (powdered) sugar

Preheat the oven to 180°C (160°C Fan) 350°F, Gas Mark 4. Lightly grease 4 compartments in a mini bundt tin and dust the pan with flour, tapping out any excess.

Place the sugar and lemon zest in a large bowl and rub them together with your fingertips until the mixture feels like damp sand and is intensely fragrant. Pour in the olive oil, vanilla, egg white and sour cream and whisk to form a smooth batter. In a separate bowl, whisk together the flour, baking powder and salt. Pour the oil mixture into the flour mixture and stir together briefly, just until a smooth batter forms.

Divide one-third of the batter between the greased tin compartments and top with half the raspberries, placing them in the middle of the batter and trying to prevent them from touching the metal of the pan. Spoon another third of the batter over the berries, and add the remaining berries as before. Cover with the remaining batter. Bake for 17–18 minutes, or until the cakes spring back to a light touch. Set aside to cool in the tin for a few minutes, before inverting onto a wire rack to cool completely.

To make the glaze, place the raspberries in a small saucepan and mash with a fork. Add the sugar, bring to a simmer over a medium heat and cook for 2 minutes. Pass this mixture through a fine mesh sieve, pressing with the back of a spoon extract as much juice as possible. Sift in the icing sugar a little at a time, and whisk until a thick but pourable glaze forms. Spoon over the cakes, allowing it to drip down the sides. Decorate with a few extra raspberries and a few dried cornflowers.

The glazed bundts are best served within 2 days of baking, but the unglazed cakes can also be frozen for up to a month.

Blueberry Hazelnut Ricotta Snack Cake

MAKES 4–6 SERVINGS

As far as I'm concerned, rye flour is a secret weapon in baking because it boosts the flavour of everything it's added to. This cake is ricotta-based, meaning it will stay moist for days, and it really highlights the rye flavour. Paired with hazelnuts and blueberries, it's a lightly sweet snack cake, perfect when you want something quick and easy to make.

Butter, for greasing

50g (1¾oz/⅓ cup + 1 tablespoon) plain (all-purpose) flour

50g (1¾oz/½ cup) wholemeal (wholewheat) rye flour

¾ teaspoon baking powder

¼ teaspoon bicarbonate of soda (baking soda)

1¼ teaspoons fine sea salt

125g (4½oz/½ cup + 2 tablespoons) caster (superfine or granulated) sugar

85g (3oz/⅓ cup + 2 teaspoons) ricotta cheese

1 large egg

25g (1oz/¼ cup) hazelnuts, roughly chopped

125g (4½oz/⅔ cup) blueberries

Demerara sugar, for sprinkling (optional)

Preheat the oven to 180°C (160°C Fan) 350°F, Gas Mark 4. Lightly grease a 23 x 13cm (9 x 5in) loaf tin and line it with a strip of parchment paper that overhangs the long sides, securing it in place with metal binder clips.

Place the flours in a bowl and mix in the baking powder, bicarbonate of soda, salt and sugar. In another bowl, whisk together the ricotta and egg. Add this mixture to the flour bowl and stir together gently until a smooth batter forms. Scrape into the prepared tin and spread evenly. Sprinkle with the hazelnuts and blueberries and, if you like, a little demerara sugar for additional texture and sweetness.

Bake for about 35 minutes, or until a skewer inserted into the middle comes out clean. Set aside to cool in the pan for about 15 minutes, before using the parchment paper to lift onto a wire rack to cool completely.

If stored in a sealed container, the cake will keep for 2–3 days. Slices can also be frozen for up to a month.

DESSERTS

Caramelized Banana Pudding

MAKES 4 SERVINGS

When it comes to bananas and baking, people tend to gravitate straight to banana bread, but I think it's high time we give the classic banana pudding another chance at the No.1 spot. For those unfamiliar with this American dish, it is a rich vanilla custard, layered with bananas and whipped cream. In my version, the custard is flavoured with caramelized banana and layered with whipped cream, dulce de leche and more banana. To add some texture, when I am in the US I also layer Nilla wafers into the dessert. These classic American cookies go a little soft, as in a trifle, so sponge fingers can be used instead.

1 large ripe banana, sliced

35g (1¼oz/2 tablespoons + 1 teaspoon) light brown sugar

35g (1¼oz/2 tablespoons + 1 teaspoon) unsalted butter

Pinch of sea salt flakes

300ml (10fl oz/1¼ cups) whole milk

75g (2¾oz/¼ cup + 2 tablespoons) caster (superfine or granulated) sugar

25g (1oz/3 tablespoons) cornflour (cornstarch)

1 large egg

2 large egg yolks

1 teaspoon vanilla bean paste

TO ASSEMBLE

240ml (8½fl oz/1 cup) double (heavy) cream

1 teaspoon vanilla bean paste

2 tablespoons condensed milk

1 large ripe banana, sliced

100g (3½oz) Nilla wafers or sponge fingers, broken into small pieces

4 heaped tablespoons dulce de leche

Place the banana, brown sugar, butter and salt in a saucepan over a medium heat for about 5 minutes, stirring occasionally, until the sugar has melted and the banana has become soft and caramelized. Transfer the mixture to a bowl and set aside.

Place the milk and half the caster sugar in the empty saucepan over a medium heat and bring to a simmer. Meanwhile, place the remaining sugar and the cornflour in a large bowl and whisk to combine. Add the egg, the yolks and vanilla and whisk until smooth. Pour in the heated milk while whisking to prevent curdling, then return the mixture to the pan. Place over a medium heat and whisk constantly until bubbling and thick. Continue heating for another minute or so to ensure the starch is cooked out, then transfer to a bowl. Using either a fork or a stick blender, mash or blend the banana mixture into a rough purée and stir into the custard. Refrigerate until needed; it will keep for a couple of days.

To assemble the dessert, place the cream, vanilla and condensed milk in a bowl and whisk just until the mixture holds soft peaks. Add the chilled custard to a separate bowl and beat until smooth. Layer the wafers, custard, banana, dulce de leche and cream into small glasses, making 2 separate layers of each ingredient. Chill until required. You can serve the dessert immediately after assembly, but allowing the wafers to sit and soften slightly creates a more comforting texture.

Mango Pudding

MAKES 2–4 SERVINGS

The Japanese pudding, or 'purin', that inspired this dessert is very similar to crème caramel or flan, a set custard with a caramel topping. There are two versions – one set with eggs and one set with gelatine, the latter being more common in shop-bought versions. The super-easy recipe below is made with both eggs and gelatine and requires no baking. The creamy dessert can be made with fresh mangoes when in season (see note below) or canned mango purée at other times.

1½ sheets of gelatine

50ml (2fl oz/3 tablespoons + 1 teaspoon) double (heavy) cream

150ml (5fl oz/½ cup + 2 tablespoons) mango purée

2 large eggs

50g (1¾oz/¼ cup) caster (superfine or granulated) sugar

Juice of ½ lime

Diced mango, to serve (optional)

FOR THE LIME CARAMEL

50g (1¾oz/¼ cup) caster (superfine or granulated) sugar

1 tablespoon boiling water

30ml (1fl oz/2 tablespoons) lime juice

First make the lime caramel: place the sugar in a small pan over a medium heat, stirring occasionally, until melted and caramelized. Add the boiling water and swirl to combine. Add the lime juice, and heat for another minute, or until the caramel is smooth. Pour into 2 x 250ml (9fl oz) ramekins or dariole moulds (or 4 smaller ones if you prefer). Set aside.

To make the custard, place the gelatine sheets in a bowl and cover with ice-cold water. Place the cream and mango purée in a saucepan over a medium heat and bring to a simmer. Meanwhile, place the eggs and sugar in a bowl and whisk to combine. Once the mango has come to a simmer, pour it over the eggs, whisking to prevent them from scrambling. Return this mixture to the saucepan, place over a medium heat and stir constantly, until the custard coats the back of a spoon and reaches around 75°C (167°F). Take off the heat. Squeeze the gelatine dry, then add to the custard, stirring until dissolved. Set the custard aside to cool for 10 minutes, before stirring in the lime juice.

Pour the custard into the ramekins and refrigerate, preferably overnight, but for at least 4 hours, until set.

To serve, dip the dishes briefly into a bowl of hot water to loosen the puddings, then invert onto plates and serve with a little diced mango if you wish.

NOTE If making the mango purée yourself, cut a little more than 150g (5½oz) mango into small cubes and purée in a blender until smooth. The finished texture should be free-flowing and pourable; if too thick, you can thin it with a little lime juice. Pass the purée through a fine mesh sieve before using.

Strawberry and Mascarpone Pots

MAKES 4 SERVINGS

Not quite a trifle and not quite a tiramisu, this recipe borrows from both. It was inspired by the strawberry and mascarpone dessert served at Da Enzo in Rome, a gloriously rich mascarpone cream topped with wild strawberries. Served in a tiny glass, it is the perfect end to a meal. My version keeps the thick mascarpone cream and strawberries, but I have also added sponge fingers drizzled with elderflower liqueur, a nod to the great British trifle.

200g (7oz) strawberries, hulled and diced

2 teaspoons caster (superfine or granulated) sugar

80g (2¾oz) sponge fingers (about 8)

90ml (3¼fl oz/8 tablespoons) elderflower liqueur, preferably St Germain

FOR THE MASCARPONE CREAM

3 large egg yolks

50g (1¾oz/¼ cup) caster (superfine or granulated) sugar

225g (8oz) mascarpone, at room temperature

1 teaspoon vanilla bean paste

Place the strawberries in a small bowl and stir in the sugar. Set aside for 30–60 minutes to macerate.

To make the mascarpone cream, place the egg yolks and sugar in a heatproof bowl set over a pan of simmering water. Whisk constantly for about 5 minutes, or until the mixture is thick and pale, akin to a homemade mayonnaise. Remove the bowl from the pan and whisk for a minute or so to cool slightly. Add the mascarpone and vanilla paste and continue whisking until smooth and creamy. Set aside.

To assemble the desserts, break up half the sponge fingers and place them in the bottom of 4 small glasses. Drizzle a tablespoon of the elderflower liqueur into each glass. Using a quarter of the strawberries, spoon them over the sponges, then top with half the mascarpone cream. Make a second layer in the same way. You should be left with half the strawberries. Place these and the desserts in the refrigerator for at least 4 hours, until the cream is set and the sponge fingers have softened slightly. Top with the remaining strawberries just before serving.

These desserts are best eaten within 2 days of making.

Lemon and Pistachio Posset

MAKES 2 SERVINGS

While the flavours of lemon and pistachio give a decidedly Italian vibe to this dish, it is firmly rooted in a classic British dessert called lemon posset. It is made by curdling cream with lemon juice, but the result is silky smooth. The pistachio spread used to top the dessert is generally available from Italian delis, but chocolate hazelnut spread can be used instead, a surprising but delicious pairing with the lemon.

225ml (8fl oz/¾ cup + 3 tablespoons) double (heavy) cream

60g (2¼oz/¼ cup + 1 tablespoon) caster (superfine or granulated) sugar

2 lemons, 1 zested

TO SERVE

1 heaped tablespoon pistachio spread

Chopped pistachios

Place the cream, sugar and lemon zest in a small pan over a medium heat and whisk constantly as the mixture comes to a simmer. Heat for a further minute, then pour into a jug.

Slice the lemons in half, squeeze out the juice and measure 65ml (2½fl oz/¼ cup + 1 teaspoon) into the jug, whisking as you do so. Pour the posset into 2 small glasses. If you prefer the dessert without the added texture of lemon zest, strain through a fine mesh sieve as you pour. Refrigerate for 3–4 hours, or until set.

To serve, place half the pistachio spread on top of each dessert and smooth with the back of the spoon. Sprinkle with a few chopped pistachios and serve immediately, or store in the refrigerator for up to 2 days.

Sour Cherry with Rye Hazelnut Crumble

MAKES 2–4 SERVINGS

Crumble, for me, is food of the gods, and absolute perfection when served with cold custard or vanilla ice cream. This version, made with sour cherries topped with a rye flour, oat and hazelnut crumble, is a fabulously warming winter dessert. I buy frozen sour cherries, which are easier to find than fresh ones, and are so useful to have on hand when a longing for crumble overtakes you. As the recipe is so simple, I always make a double batch of the crumble mixture and freeze the unused half for a future occasion (no need to defrost).

300g (10½oz) frozen sour cherries

2 tablespoons caster (superfine or granulated) sugar

2 drops of almond extract (optional)

FOR THE CRUMBLE TOPPING

75g (2¾oz/¾ cup) wholemeal (wholewheat) rye flour

50g (1¾oz/¼ cup) caster (superfine or granulated) sugar

65g (2½oz/4½ tablespoons) unsalted butter, diced and chilled

40g (1½oz/½ cup) rolled oats

40g (1½oz/⅓ cup) chopped toasted hazelnuts

Preheat the oven to 190°C (170°C Fan) 375°F, Gas Mark 5.

Place the cherries, sugar and almond extract (if using) in a 750ml (27fl oz) ovenproof baking dish and stir to combine.

To make the crumble, place the flour and sugar in a bowl and mix together. Add the butter and toss to coat. Rub together with your fingertips until it starts to form clumps and you can no longer see any distinct chunks of butter. Add the oats and hazelnuts, and stir to distribute evenly. Scatter the crumble mixture over the fruit.

Transfer the dish to a baking tray (cookie sheet) and bake for 35–40 minutes, until the crumble is golden and the fruit is bubbling.

Serve immediately. Any leftovers can be refrigerated and served up to a couple of days later. Cover in foil and reheat at 190°C (170°C Fan) 375°F, Gas Mark 5 for about 20 minutes, or until hot. I also love to eat the leftovers cold.

Peanut Butter Chocolate Fondants

MAKES 2

Who can deny the lure of a chocolate fondant? It may be a bit clichéd these days, but that's only because it became so ubiquitous for a time, when every restaurant seemed to have a version on the menu. This fondant, a perfect date night dessert, is completely classic, apart from the peanut butter added to the chocolate centre to give the flavour of a peanut butter cup. I like to serve it with vanilla ice cream for a lovely hot/cold contrast, or with raspberry sorbet to suggest the flavours of a peanut butter and jelly sandwich.

70g (2½oz/5 tablespoons) unsalted butter, diced, plus extra for greasing

70g (2½oz) dark chocolate (65–70% cocoa solids)

50g (1¾oz/scant ¼ cup) light brown sugar

2 large eggs

2 teaspoons cocoa powder

50g (1¾oz/⅓ cup + 1 tablespoon) plain (all-purpose) flour

Pinch of fine sea salt

2 heaped teaspoons smooth or crunchy peanut butter

Preheat the oven to 180°C (160°C Fan) 350°F, Gas Mark 4. Lightly grease 2 x 250ml (9fl oz) ramekins or dariole moulds and set them on a baking tray (cookie sheet).

Place the butter and chocolate in a bowl set over a pan of simmering water and stir occasionally until fully melted. Set aside.

Place the sugar and eggs in another bowl and whisk together for 2 minutes. Pour into the slightly cooled chocolate mixture, stirring with the whisk until fully combined. Sift in the cocoa powder, flour and salt, then mix together until a batter forms. Divide equally between the prepared dishes and top each one with a heaped teaspoon of peanut butter.

Bake for 8 minutes, until the edges are puffed but the centre still seems a little moist. Invert immediately onto serving plates and serve with a scoop of vanilla ice cream or raspberry sorbet.

NOTE The fondants can be prepared up to 24 hours ahead and refrigerated until you're ready to bake; they can also be frozen for up to a month if unbaked. If baking them straight from the refrigerator, add an extra minute in the oven. If baking from frozen, add an extra 3–5 minutes. Once baked, they should be served immediately.

Cherries Jubilee Crêpes

MAKES 2 SERVINGS

There is something I love about retro desserts: think baked Alaska, Black Forest gateau or pineapple upside-down cake. They became popular for good reason, even if their heyday has passed. This dessert is a mash-up of two other retro classics – cherries jubilee and crêpes Suzette. Serve with plenty of vanilla ice cream for dessert heaven.

75g (2¾oz/½ cup + 2 tablespoons) plain (all-purpose) flour

15g (½oz/1 tablespoon) caster (superfine or granulated) sugar

Pinch of fine sea salt

160ml (5½fl oz/⅔ cup) whole milk

1 large egg

15g (½oz/1 tablespoon) unsalted butter, melted and cooled

Vegetable oil, for greasing

FOR THE CHERRY COMPOTE

125g (4¼oz) sweet cherries, halved and pitted

2 tablespoons caster (superfine or granulated) sugar

4 tablespoons kirsch or white rum

Place the flour, sugar and salt in a large bowl and whisk to combine. Make a well in the centre, add the milk, egg and butter, and whisk until a smooth batter forms. Set aside to rest for 30 minutes.

Meanwhile, place the cherries and sugar in a small saucepan and cook over a medium heat until the fruit has become juicy. Pour in the kirsch and heat for about 5 more minutes, or until the liquid has become a little syrupy. Set aside.

When the batter has rested, place a 23–25cm (9–10in) crêpe pan or frying pan over a medium heat and wipe with some oiled kitchen paper. Pour in a small ladleful of batter, swirling it around to coat the base of pan thinly and evenly. Cook for 45–60 seconds per side, until golden. Transfer to a serving platter, fold into quarters and keep warm while you cook the remaining crêpes. Remember to oil the pan for each one.

To serve, top the crêpes with the warm cherry compote and a few scoops of vanilla ice cream.

Hazelnut Profiteroles with Coffee Ice Cream

MAKES 4 SERVINGS

Once you've mastered choux pastry, profiteroles are a very easy dessert to whip up. This version of the classic French dessert is made with a fabulous no-churn coffee ice cream, inspired by Nigella Lawson's excellent recipe, and the choux buns themselves are sprinkled liberally with hazelnuts. To serve, a warm and rich milk chocolate sauce is poured over the profiteroles.

1 batch Choux Pastry (see page 156)

1 large egg, beaten

100g (3½oz/¾ cup + 2 tablespoons) finely chopped hazelnuts

FOR THE NO-CHURN COFFEE ICE CREAM

1 tablespoon instant espresso powder

150ml (5fl oz/½ cup + 2 tablespoons) double (heavy) cream

85g (3oz/4 tablespoons + 1 teaspoon) condensed milk

2 tablespoons hazelnut liqueur

FOR THE CHOCOLATE SAUCE

100g (3½oz) milk chocolate, finely chopped

180ml (6¼fl oz/¾ cup) double (heavy) cream

First make the ice cream: place the espresso powder in a small pan and pour in a third of the cream. Place over a medium heat and bring to a simmer, stirring to dissolve the coffee. Refrigerate until cool.

Pour the cooled coffee cream into a large bowl, add the remaining cream, the condensed milk and hazelnut liqueur and whisk just until the mixture holds very soft peaks. Scrape into a sealable container and freeze for at least 4 hours, or until firm.

Preheat the oven to 190ºC (170ºC Fan) 375ºF, Gas Mark 5. Line a baking tray (cookie sheet) with parchment paper.

Spoon the choux pastry into a piping bag fitted with a small round piping tip. Pipe as many 3cm (1¼in) balls as you can onto your prepared tray. Lightly brush them with a little beaten egg and sprinkle liberally with the chopped hazelnuts. Bake for about 25 minutes, until dry and crisp. Turn off the heat and allow the choux to cool down for about 30 minutes before removing from the oven.

To make the sauce, place the chocolate and cream in a small saucepan over a medium heat and stir constantly until completely smooth. Pour into a jug.

To assemble, use a serrated knife to slice the profiteroles in half. Place a small scoop of the ice cream in each half and sandwich them back together. Serve them on 4 individual plates, offering the sauce jug alongside, or pile them into a pyramid on a large platter and pour the sauce over, allowing everyone to serve themselves.

Once baked, the choux buns can be stored in a sealed container for a couple of days. The ice cream can be made up to a week in advance.

Mum's Trifle Made Mini

MAKES 4 SERVINGS

There is a joke in my family that no one will visit for Christmas unless my mum makes one of her trifles. In fact, there's likely to be two of them in the refrigerator to satisfy everyone's desire for it. Her recipe is a spin on the classic sherry trifle, so it's boozy and never contains jelly, but she does add a touch of almond extract and sometimes crisp amaretti biscuits to add a hit of almond flavour that goes brilliantly with the raspberries. This is a downsized version of that recipe, a true taste of home. If you fancy the idea of using amaretti, I suggest going 50:50 with sponge fingers for a great mix of taste and texture.

80g (2¾oz/¼ cup) raspberry jam, shop-bought or homemade (see page 164)

3 tablespoons sweet sherry

⅛ teaspoon almond extract

100g (3½oz) raspberries

70g (2½oz) sponge fingers (about 10), broken into chunks

240ml (8½fl oz/1 cup) ready-made vanilla custard

180ml (6¼fl oz/¾ cup) double (heavy) cream

Place the jam and a splash of water in a small pan over a medium heat and bring to a simmer, stirring until any lumps have broken up. Take off the heat and stir in the sherry and almond extract.

Place the raspberries in a bowl with the sponge fingers, pour over the sherry mixture and stir until the berries and sponges are fully coated. Divide equally between 4 small glasses, pressing slightly to compact a little. Top with the custard, then refrigerate while you complete the next step.

Pour the cream into a bowl and whisk just until it is holding its shape but not yet in soft peaks. (It is best to underwhip at this stage because the cream will firm up as the desserts set.) Spoon the cream on top of the trifles, then return them to the refrigerator for at least 4 hours before serving.

Once made, the trifles can be refrigerated for up to 3 days.

NOTE If you happen to have some leftover Pastry Cream (see page 161), it can be used instead of the custard. Simply warm and thin out with milk to a similar consistency.

Date Night Crème Brûlée

MAKES 2 SERVINGS

It might have only a few simple elements — a creamy custard topped with caramelized sugar — but crème brûlée is so much more than the sum of its parts. For this version I like to infuse the cream base with fresh ginger to give an underlying warmth.

225ml (8fl oz/¾ cup + 3 tablespoons) double (heavy) cream

2 tablespoons freshly grated ginger

½ teaspoon vanilla bean paste

3 large egg yolks

40g (1½oz/3 tablespoons) light brown sugar

Caster or granulated sugar, for the topping

Pour the cream into a small saucepan and add the ginger. Place over a medium heat and bring to a simmer, then continue heating for another 2 minutes. Cover the pan and set aside to infuse for at least 1 hour. If you have time, allow the cream to cool, then leave to infuse overnight in the refrigerator.

Preheat the oven to 140ºC (120ºC Fan) 275ºF, Gas Mark 1. Set out a baking dish, about 300ml (10fl oz) in capacity.

Add the vanilla to the infused cream, place the pan over a medium heat and bring back to a simmer.

Meanwhile, place the egg yolks and brown sugar in a large bowl and whisk to combine. Pour the warmed cream into the egg mixture, whisking gently to prevent the yolks from scrambling. Pour through a fine mesh sieve into your baking dish (this will remove the ginger). Place in a roasting tray and transfer to the oven. Pour in enough hot water to reach about halfway up the side of the baking dish. Bake for about 40 minutes, or until the crème is set around the edges but has a gelatinous wobble in the middle. Remove the tray from the oven and allow the crème to cool in it for an hour or so before transferring it to the refrigerator to chill for at least 4 hours.

When ready to serve, sprinkle a thin, even layer of caster sugar over the crème and caramelize it with a blowtorch or under a hot grill (broiler). To balance the sweetness, I like to go dark with the caramelizing, but feel free to take it to the colour that you prefer. Allow to cool for a couple of minutes before serving.

NOTE   The baked crème can be refrigerated for a couple of days before use, but once the sugar has been added and brûléed, the dessert should be served soon after; it could be refrigerated for a couple hours, but no more.

Vegan Baked Alaska

MAKES 6 SERVINGS

When my oldest brother was growing up, baked Alaska was the dessert he had each and every birthday. Traditionally, it is made with a cake base, ice cream and torched meringue. In my family there was also fruit added, normally raspberries. My version is not quite traditional, as it's fully vegan, and it also includes fruit in the form of raspberry sorbet. A great advantage of this dish is that it can be prepared up to a month in advance, leaving only a little work to do before serving.

40ml (1½fl oz/2 tablespoons + 2 teaspoons) vegetable oil, plus extra for greasing

30g (1oz/2 tablespoons) light brown sugar

85g (3oz/¼ cup) golden syrup

50ml (2fl oz/3 tablespoons + 1 teaspoon) soya milk

85g (3oz/⅔ cup) plain (all-purpose) flour

¼ teaspoon bicarbonate of soda (baking soda)

¼ teaspoon fine sea salt

1 teaspoon apple cider vinegar

500ml (18fl oz) raspberry sorbet or vegan ice cream

FOR THE VEGAN SWISS MERINGUE

150ml (5fl oz/½ cup + 2 tablespoons) aquafaba (the liquid from a can of chickpeas/garbanzos)

100g (3½oz/½ cup) caster (superfine or granulated) sugar

1 teaspoon vanilla bean paste

Pinch of fine sea salt

½ teaspoon cream of tartar

Preheat the oven to 180ºC (160ºC Fan) 350ºF, Gas Mark 4. Lightly grease a rimmed 23 x 15cm (9 x 6in) baking tray (eighth sheet pan) and line the base with parchment paper.

Place the oil, sugar, golden syrup and soya milk in a small saucepan over a medium heat and stir frequently until the sugar has dissolved. Set aside.

Place the flour, bicarbonate of soda and salt in a large bowl and mix together. Pour in the syrup mixture and the vinegar and whisk until a smooth batter forms. Pour into the prepared tray and spread evenly. Bake for 13–15 minutes, or until the cake springs back to a light touch. Set aside to cool in the tray for 15 minutes, before transferring to a wire rack to cool completely.

To assemble the dessert, line a 23 x 13cm (9 x 5in) loaf tin with clingfilm (plastic wrap), letting it overhang the sides. Scoop the sorbet into the tin and set aside for a few minutes, until it becomes spreadable. Use the back of a spoon to spread evenly. Trim the cake so it fits the tin and sits neatly on top of the sorbet. Fold the overhanging clingfilm over the cake, then wrap the loaf tin in another sheet of clingfilm and freeze for at least 4 hours, or until needed. It can be frozen for up to a month.

To make the meringue, place the aquafaba, sugar, vanilla and salt in a small saucepan over a medium heat and bring to a simmer, stirring occasionally. Continue simmering for 10 minutes. Pour into a large bowl, add the cream of tartar, and whisk with an electric mixer for about 10 minutes, or until a stiff meringue forms.

To serve the dessert, use the clingfilm to lift it from the tin and invert onto a serving platter. Spread the meringue all over the dessert, then brown with a blowtorch or under a hot grill (broiler). Serve immediately.

One Egg Pavlova for Two

MAKES 2 SERVINGS

I love pavlova for its simplicity and for the lack of hands-on time required. When making one, though, it's really important to ensure the egg white and sugar are properly whisked so that the sugar is dissolved. If not, the sugar can weep from the baked meringue. As for the topping, you can use custard, whipped cream or even ice cream, and whatever fruit you prefer.

1 large egg white

Pinch of cream of tartar

Pinch of fine sea salt

60g (2¼oz/¼ cup + 1 tablespoon) caster (superfine or granulated) sugar

½ teaspoon cornflour (cornstarch)

½ teaspoon vanilla bean paste

2 drops of lemon juice

FOR THE TOPPING

150g (5½oz/½ cup + 2 tablespoons) double (heavy) cream, lightly whipped

200g (7oz) fresh fruit

Icing (powdered) sugar, for dusting

Preheat the oven to 120°C (100°C Fan) 250°F, Gas Mark ½. Line a baking tray (cookie sheet) with parchment paper.

Place the egg white, cream of tartar and salt in a bowl and whisk until foamy. While continuing to whisk, slowly add the sugar a little at a time. Whisk until the sugar has dissolved and the meringue holds stiff, glossy peaks. Add the cornflour, vanilla and lemon juice and whisk briefly to combine.

Scrape the meringue into a mound on the prepared tray and spread into a circle roughly 12cm (5in) wide with a slight well in the middle.

Bake for about 1½ hours, or until dry and crisp. Turn off the oven and allow the pavlova to cool inside for at least 1 hour. (I often leave it in there overnight.)

To serve, add your choice of toppings and dust with icing sugar (the whipped cream and fruit listed here are a rough guide to the amounts needed).

Once assembled, the pavlova is best served on the same day, but the meringue element can be made a day or two in advance if required.

BREADS AND BUNS

Dulce de Leche Pain Suisse

MAKES 6 SERVINGS

Pain Suisse (also known as brioche Suisse) is a delightful French pastry that is criminally underappreciated. Thankfully, it is slowly becoming more popular, with more bakeries (at least in the UK) making their own versions, often using croissant dough instead of the more traditional brioche. My version uses a dulce de leche-enriched pastry cream and plenty of chocolate chips.

75g (2¾oz/¼ cup) dulce de leche

½ batch Pastry Cream (see page 161)

1 tablespoon cornflour (cornstarch)

1 tablespoon milk

Flour, for dusting

1 batch Brioche Dough (see page 158), refrigerated overnight

75g (2¾oz/scant ½ cup) chocolate chips

1 large egg, beaten

Beat the dulce de leche into the pastry cream until smooth. Place the cornflour and milk in a small bowl and whisk together. Pour into the pastry cream and whisk to combine. Transfer to a saucepan over a medium heat and whisk constantly, until thickened and bubbling. Pour into a bowl and refrigerate for 1 hour.

Line 2 baking trays (cookie sheets) with parchment paper. Lightly flour a work surface and roll the dough into a 35 x 30cm (14 x 12in) rectangle. With a short side directly in front of you, spread the pastry cream over the lower half of the rectangle. Sprinkle with the chocolate chips, then fold the uncovered dough over the filling, pressing down lightly to seal. Using a sharp knife, cut the dough into 6 equal slices and carefully lift onto the prepared tray(s). Cover lightly with clingfilm (plastic wrap) and set aside for 1–2 hours, until the slices have doubled in thickness.

Preheat the oven to 190ºC (170ºC Fan) 375ºF, Gas Mark 5. Brush the tops of the slices with a little beaten egg, then bake for 10–15 minutes, or until golden brown. Set aside until cool.

These little breads are best served on the day they are made, but if stored in a sealed container will be good for a day or two after baking. They can also be frozen for up to a month, then defrosted and lightly warmed through in the oven.

NOTE For a simpler version of this recipe, use just the pastry cream and chocolate chips, omitting the dulce de leche and cornflour steps.

Strawberry Maritozzi

MAKES 6

In Rome, hidden behind the Coliseum and away from the crowds of tourists, is the bakery Pasticceria Regoli, and it was here I had my first taste of maritozzi, a type of brioche bun flavoured with a hint of citrus and honey, and generously filled with whipped cream. Simple but elegant. The story goes that these buns were given as tokens of affection, or even as an engagement gift from men to their partners, which gave the buns their name – *marito* is Italian for 'husband'. My version below includes macerated strawberries, adding a hint of British summer.

1 batch Brioche Dough, made with 2 tablespoons honey instead of the sugar, and the zest of 1 orange added with the milk (see page 158)

1 large egg, beaten

FOR THE FILLING

250g (9oz) strawberries

1½ tablespoon caster (superfine or granulated) sugar

¼ teaspoon vanilla bean paste

300ml (10fl oz/1¼ cups) double (heavy) cream, whipped to soft peaks

Divide the chilled dough into 6 equal pieces and roll each into a ball. Lightly cover with a clean tea towel (dishtowel) and leave for 15 minutes. Meanwhile, line a baking tray (cookie sheet) with parchment paper.

Gently roll each ball of dough into a stubby oval, looking almost like a small potato. Place on the prepared tray, lightly cover with clingfilm (plastic wrap) and set aside for an hour or so, until doubled in size.

Preheat the oven to 180ºC (160ºC Fan) 350ºF, Gas Mark 4. Brush the risen buns with the beaten egg, then bake for 15–17 minutes, or until deep golden brown. Set aside to cool.

To make the filling, hull and quarter the strawberries, reserving 2 whole berries for decoration. Place the quartered strawberries in a bowl with the sugar and vanilla, toss together and set aside for 1 hour.

To serve, slice the brioche buns through the middle, but leave them hinged together, like a book. Spoon some of the strawberries into the buns, close to the 'hinge', then fill with whipped cream, smoothing it so it's flush with the opening of the buns. Cut each reserved strawberry into 3 slices and place a slice on the exposed cream of each bun.

These are best eaten on the day they are assembled, but the buns can be baked a day in advance if necessary.

Chocolate and Espresso Brioche Buns

MAKES 6

While you can serve these buns at any time of day, I find them especially good for an indulgent brunch. As the brioche dough is easier to work with after an overnight rise in the refrigerator, it makes sense to use it in the morning and serve the buns warm from the oven with strong black coffee to accompany them.

Flour, for dusting

1 batch Brioche Dough (see page 158)

FOR THE FILLING

50g (1¾oz) dark chocolate (65–75% cocoa solids), finely chopped

70g (2½oz/5 tablespoons) unsalted butter, diced

2 tablespoons instant espresso powder

1 tablespoon cocoa powder

30g (1oz/2 tablespoons) light brown sugar

Large pinch of fine sea salt

FOR THE GLAZE

100g (3½oz/⅓ cup + 2 tablespoons) cream cheese, at room temperature

30g (1oz/2 tablespoons) unsalted butter, at room temperature

120g (4¼oz/1 cup) icing (powdered) sugar

2 tablespoons dark maple syrup

1 teaspoon vanilla bean paste

Pinch of fine sea salt

To make the filling, place the chocolate, butter and coffee powder in a heatproof bowl set over a pan of simmering water and melt together, stirring occasionally. Take the bowl off the heat, add the remaining filling ingredients and stir to combine. Set aside.

Line a 23 x 15cm (9 x 6in) rimmed baking tray (eighth sheet pan) with parchment paper. Lightly flour a work surface and roll the brioche dough into a rectangle about 25 x 40cm (10 x 16in). Spread the filling over it evenly, taking it right to the edges. Wait a couple of minutes, until the filling goes slightly tacky, before rolling it into a log, starting from one of the shorter sides. Cut into 6 equal pieces and place on the prepared tray. Lightly cover the buns with clingfilm (plastic wrap) and set aside for 1 hour, or until doubled in size.

When ready, preheat the oven to 190°C (170°C Fan) 375°F, Gas Mark 5. Bake the buns for 25–30 minutes, or until golden brown, then set aside to cool.

Place the glaze ingredients in a large bowl and mix until smooth. The consistency should be thick but just about pourable. Spoon the glaze onto the buns and spread over the surface.

If stored in a sealed container, the buns will keep for 2–3 days, but they are best eaten on the day they are made, while still just a touch warm from the oven.

Rhubarb and Marzipan Cream Buns

MAKES 6

My favourite Swedish bake, Semla — a cardamom-flavoured brioche bun filled with marzipan and cream – is the inspiration behind this recipe. I go a step further here, combining fragrant cardamom with sweet and sharp rhubarb (ideally forced English rhubarb), and using it to fill the buns alongside the marzipan and cream. Heaven!

1 batch Brioche Dough, made with 1 teaspoon freshly ground cardamom added to the flour (see page 158)

1 large egg, beaten

100g (3½oz) marzipan, broken into small pieces

300ml (10fl oz/1¼ cups) double (heavy) cream

Icing (powdered) sugar, for dusting

FOR THE ROASTED RHUBARB

240g (8¾oz) rhubarb, cut into pieces 2cm (¾in) long

50g (1¾oz/¼ cup) caster (superfine or granulated) sugar

1 teaspoon vanilla bean paste

1 tablespoon lemon juice

Line a baking tray (cookie sheet) with parchment paper. Divide the brioche dough into 6 equal pieces and roll each into a ball. Place on the prepared tray, lightly cover with clingfilm (plastic wrap) and set aside for an hour or so, until doubled in size.

Meanwhile, preheat the oven to 190ºC (170ºC Fan) 375ºF, Gas Mark 5. Place the rhubarb in a small rimmed baking tray (an eighth sheet pan is ideal), sprinkle with the sugar, vanilla and lemon juice and stir to combine. Bake for about 15 minutes, or until the rhubarb is soft but still holding its shape. Set aside until cold.

Once the dough has risen, reheat the oven to 190ºC (170ºC Fan) 375ºF, Gas Mark 5. Brush the buns with a little beaten egg and bake for about 15 minutes, or until golden brown. Set aside to cool.

To assemble, use a serrated knife to slice the tops off the buns, then use your fingers to pull out a little of the dough. Divide the marzipan between the buns and top with the rhubarb and its syrup. Whisk the cream in a bowl until it just holds soft peaks. Spoon or pipe the cream over the rhubarb and place the brioche 'lids' back on top. Dust with a little icing sugar.

Once assembled, the buns are best eaten on the day they are made, but the unfilled buns can be stored in a sealed container for 2 days, or frozen for up to a month.

Everything Bagel Morning Buns

MAKES 6

These savoury morning buns are filled with a cheese sauce, sprinkled with bacon and spring onions, and after baking are brushed with a little butter and sprinkled liberally with Everything Bagel Seasoning, a ready-made condiment that is also very easy to make yourself. They are an ode to breakfast in New York.

Flour, for dusting

1 batch Brioche Dough (see page 158)

1 large egg, beaten

1 tablespoon unsalted butter, melted

FOR THE FILLING

25g (1oz/1 tablespoon + 2 teaspoons) unsalted butter, at room temperature

2 tablespoons plain (all-purpose) flour

250ml (9fl oz/1 cup + 2 teaspoons) whole milk

125g (4½oz/1 cup) grated Cheddar cheese

1 tablespoon Dijon mustard

200g (7oz) pancetta, diced and cooked until crisp

2 spring onions (scallions), sliced

FOR THE BAGEL SEASONING

2 tablespoons poppy seeds

2 tablespoons white sesame seeds

1 tablespoon black sesame seeds

1 tablespoon dried garlic flakes

1 tablespoon dried onion flakes

1 teaspoon sea salt flakes

First make the filling: melt the butter in a saucepan over a medium heat, and continue heating until it starts to foam. Add the flour, stirring to form a paste, then cook for 2 minutes, stirring frequently. Pour in the milk a little at time, stirring until the mixture is smooth before adding more. Once all the milk has been added, simmer until the sauce has thickened, about 5 minutes. Add the cheese and mustard, stirring until the sauce is smooth again. Pour into a heatproof container, press a sheet of clingfilm (plastic wrap) directly onto the surface and refrigerate until fully chilled, about 4 hours.

When the sauce is cold, line a 23 x 15cm (9 x 6in) rimmed baking tray (an eighth sheet pan) with parchment paper. Lightly flour the work surface and roll the brioche dough into a rectangle about 25 x 40cm (10 x 16in). Spread the cheese filling all over it, then sprinkle evenly with the pancetta and spring onions. Roll up the dough, starting from one of the shorter edges. Cut the log into 6 equal slices and place on the prepared tray. Cover lightly with clingfilm and set aside for 1 hour, or until doubled in size.

Meanwhile, combine all the bagel seasoning ingredients in a jar and shake well. If kept sealed, the mixture will keep for months. You'll only need a little for this recipe, but it's great for seasoning all manner of things, especially brunch-time dishes.

Once the buns have proved, preheat the oven to 190ºC (170ºC Fan) 375ºF, Gas Mark 5. Brush the top of the buns with the beaten egg, then bake for about 25 minutes, or until golden. Set aside for 5 minutes before brushing with the melted butter and sprinkling liberally with the bagel seasoning.

The buns are best served warm, but if stored in a sealed container can be served up to 2 days after baking. They can also be separated and frozen individually for up to 2 months.

Crumpets

MAKES 4

The joy of a crumpet lies in the little holes that cover the surface which, when toasted, hold the melted butter that is slathered over. Crumpets are not always something we consider making from scratch, but they're incredibly easy and, as with most things, so much better when homemade.

100g (3½oz/¾ cup + 1 teaspoon) strong white bread flour

65ml (2½fl oz/¼ cup + 1 teaspoon) warm water

70ml (2¾fl oz/¼ cup + 2 teaspoons) whole milk

½ teaspoon fast-action dried yeast

½ teaspoon caster (superfine or granulated) sugar

¼ teaspoon fine sea salt

¾ teaspoon baking powder

1 teaspoon cold water

Vegetable oil, for greasing

Place all but the last 3 ingredients in a large jug and whisk into a smooth batter. Set aside for 1 hour, or until the batter has increased in volume and is incredibly bubbly, looking a bit like a science experiment.

When ready, place the baking powder in a small bowl, stir in the cold water, then mix briefly into the batter.

Lightly grease a large frying pan (skillet), preferably cast iron, and lightly grease 4 x 10cm (4in) rings. You can use tart rings, crumpet rings or any form of dessert ring, but you can also do without the rings, cooking the batter like pancakes. In this form, they are known as 'pikelets'.

Place the greased rings in the pan over a low–medium heat. Divide the batter evenly between them and allow to cook until the bubbles that appear on the surface hold their shape and the batter starts to dry out and lose its shine. When almost set and the base of each crumpet is browned, flip them over and cook for another minute or so, until browned. Serve while still warm, or let them cool completely and serve later, toasted until crisp.

These are best eaten on the day they are made, spread with salted butter and honey or jam.

Classic Pretzels

MAKES 4

Although supposedly invented by an Italian monk, pretzels are most associated with Germany, where they are often eaten with mustard and a pint of beer. Germany is also where pretzels began to be dunked in a lye (caustic soda) solution before baking to give them their characteristic colour and flavour. Thankfully, bicarbonate of soda (baking soda) can be used instead of lye, and if you bake it first, the results are surprisingly good (see note).

250g (9oz/2 cups) strong white bread flour

½ teaspoon fine sea salt

3g (½ teaspoon) dried fast-action yeast

25g (1oz/2 tablespoons) unsalted butter, at room temperature

130ml (4¼fl oz/½ cup + 2 teaspoons) lukewarm water

1 tablespoon barley malt extract or honey

Vegetable oil, for greasing and brushing

Sea salt flakes, for sprinkling

FOR THE PRE-BAKING SOLUTION

1 litre (35fl oz/4 cups and 1½ tablespoons) water

50g (1¾oz/2 tablespoons + 1 teaspoon) barley malt extract

50g (1¾oz/3 tablespoons + 1 teaspoon) bicarbonate of soda (baking soda)

NOTE If the bicarbonate of soda is spread on a foil-lined tray and baked for 1 hour at 180°C (160°C) 350°F, Gas Mark 4, its pH changes, making it closer to lye, the ingredient traditionally used in solution to make pretzels chewy and a deep golden brown. The bicarbonate mixture is less caustic than lye, but you should still take care when using it and try not to get it on your skin.

Place the flour, salt and yeast in a large bowl and stir together. Add the butter and rub into the mixture until there are no visible lumps. Make a well in the centre and pour in the water and malt extract. Mix together to form a shaggy dough, then tip onto a work surface and knead until smooth and elastic, about 10 minutes. Place the dough in a lightly greased bowl, cover with clingfilm (plastic wrap) and set aside for 1–2 hours, until doubled in size.

Divide the dough into 4 equal pieces and roll them into balls. Cover and leave them to relax for 10 minutes.

Line a large baking tray (cookie sheet) with parchment paper and brush with oil or mist with a little non-stick cooking spray.

Working with 1 piece of dough at a time, roll it into a smooth rope roughly 60–65cm (24–26in) long, leaving the centre of it a little thicker than the ends. Arrange the rope in a U-shape with the ends facing you. Take both ends, cross them over once, then lift up and press onto the curved part of the rope at the top, forming the traditional pretzel shape. Transfer to the prepared tray and cover lightly with clingfilm (plastic wrap) while you make another 3 pretzels in the same way. Set aside for 30 minutes, before transferring to the refrigerator for 1 hour.

Preheat the oven to 200°C (180°C Fan) 400°F, Gas Mark 6.

To make the pre-baking solution, bring the water to the boil in a medium saucepan. Add the malt extract and bicarbonate of soda and whisk to combine. Turn the heat off, then place 1 pretzel at a time place in the liquid for 1 minute. Lift out with a slotted spoon, return to the baking tray and sprinkle liberally with sea salt flakes. Use a sharp paring knife to slit along the thicker part of the pretzels, then bake for 15–18 minutes, or until a rich mahogany brown. Leave to cool for a few minutes before eating. The pretzels will keep for up to 2 days after baking, and can be frozen for up to a month.

English Muffins

MAKES 6

If you open my freezer, you will almost always find a batch of these muffins in there, as they're a brunch staple, perfect for making a breakfast sandwich. The original recipe came to me from my friend Campbell, who's a bit of a legend in the baking world. He's the man behind much of the equipment found in bakeries across the UK and as far away as Australia. His muffin recipe is simply the best I've come across, and I am grateful to him for letting me share it with you in small batch form.

150g (5½oz/1 cup + 3 tablespoons) plain (all-purpose) flour

120g (4¼oz/scant 1 cup) strong white bread flour

1 tablespoon caster (superfine or granulated) sugar

1 teaspoon fine sea salt

1 teaspoon fast-action dried yeast

90ml (3¼fl oz/⅓ cup + 2 teaspoons) lukewarm water

90ml (3¼fl oz/⅓ cup + 2 teaspoons) whole milk

25g (1oz/1 tablespoon + 2 teaspoons) unsalted butter, melted and cooled

Coarse cornmeal, for sprinkling

Place the flours, sugar, salt and yeast in a large bowl and stir to combine. Make a well in the centre and pour in the water, milk and butter. Mix to form a shaggy dough, then turn onto a work surface and knead for about 10 minutes, or until smooth and elastic. If you like, this can be done using an electric mixer fitted with a dough hook.

Place the dough in a bowl, cover with clingfilm (plastic wrap) and set aside for 1 hour or so, until doubled in size.

Sprinkle a baking tray (cookie sheet) with coarse cornmeal. Tip the dough onto a work surface, punch down the dough, then divide into 6 equal pieces. Roll each piece into a ball and place on the prepared tray, spacing them well apart. Lightly cover with clingfilm and set aside for 45–60 minutes, until the balls have almost doubled in size.

Heat a heavy-based, preferably cast iron, frying pan (skillet) or griddle pan over a low heat. Sprinkle the top of the muffins with cornmeal and use a spatula to transfer them, top-side down, into the pan (I do half the batch at a time). Cook the muffins for about 10 minutes per side, then place in a warm oven while you cook the rest. Allow to cool for a few minutes before serving.

These muffins can be served 2–3 days after baking, but also freeze brilliantly in a plastic bag for up to 2 months.

Overnight Croque Madame Waffles

MAKES 2 SERVINGS

Most weekends I will cook brunch for my boyfriend and myself, and this overnight waffle recipe is the perfect thing when getting up, making a pot of coffee and walking the dog is more than enough activity for one day. You whip up the batter the night before so that in the morning you are ready to make waffles as quickly as it takes the waffle iron to heat up. Inspired by the classic French dish croque madame, these waffles are packed full of ham and cheese and topped with a fried egg. The amounts used here will make one large waffle per person if using a round waffle machine with deep ridges. If using a shallow machine, or one with small squares, you'll get two waffles per person.

25g (1oz/1 tablespoon + 2 teaspoons) unsalted butter, melted

150ml (5fl oz/½ cup + 2 tablespoons) whole milk

1 large egg

125g (4½oz/1 cup) plain (all-purpose) flour

1 tablespoon caster (superfine or granulated) sugar

½ teaspoon fine sea salt

1 teaspoon fast-action dried yeast

2 teaspoons English mustard powder

70g (2½oz) smoked ham, diced

75g (2¾oz/⅔ cup) grated Gruyère or Cheddar cheese

¼ teaspoon bicarbonate of soda (baking soda)

Vegetable oil, for greasing

TO SERVE

2–4 large eggs

Dried chilli flakes

Chives, finely sliced

Sea salt and freshly ground black pepper

Place the butter, milk and egg in a large jug and whisk to combine. Add the flour, sugar, salt, yeast and mustard powder and whisk briefly until a smooth batter forms. Cover and set aside for 1 hour, or until the batter is risen and very bubbly, then refrigerate overnight.

In the morning, add the ham, cheese and bicarbonate of soda to the batter. Stir until everything is evenly combined. Set aside for 10 minutes.

Meanwhile, preheat the oven to 160ºC (140ºC Fan) 325ºF, Gas Mark 3 and heat your waffle iron. Also place a wire rack on a baking tray (cookie sheet).

Lightly grease your waffle iron, then ladle in half the batter. Cook according to the manufacturer's instructions, usually for about 5 minutes, or until the waffle is golden. Transfer to the prepared tray (the wire rack will help to keep it crisp) and place in the hot oven while you cook the second waffle.

When both waffles are in the oven, fry 2 eggs, or 4 if you're catering for big appetites, seasoning them with salt, pepper and a little pinch of chilli flakes.

Serve the waffles immediately, topping them with the fried eggs and a sprinkling of chopped chives.

The basic cooked waffles can be frozen for up to a month. Simply defrost, then refresh for 10 minutes in an oven preheated to 180ºC (160ºC Fan) 350ºF, Gas Mark 4.

Smash Burgers

MAKES 2

To my mind, the best part of a burger is the crust, where the meat has browned and is rich in texture and flavour. With a smash burger, this flavour is pushed to its limit, but because it's thin and cooks so quickly, the burger remains juicy, something not easily possible with a thicker patty. You can serve the burgers with whatever toppings you prefer, but I like to keep things simple – burger sauce, pickles and a little shredded lettuce.

250g (9oz) minced (ground) beef (20% fat)

Vegetable oil, for greasing

2 Brioche Buns (see page 159)

Shredded iceberg lettuce

4 slices of American cheese (or your preferred cheese)

Sea salt and freshly ground black pepper

Sliced pickles, to serve

FOR THE QUICK BURGER SAUCE

3 tablespoons mayonnaise

2 tablespoons ketchup

First make the burger sauce: mix both ingredients for it in a small bowl, then set aside.

Divide the beef into 4 equal portions and roll into balls. Wipe a heavy, preferably cast iron or carbon steel frying pan (skillet) or griddle pan with oiled kitchen paper and place over high heat until very hot.

Slice the buns in half and place them, cut-side down, in the hot pan. Toast briefly, just until they are lightly browned. Spread the bottom halves with a little burger sauce and top with some shredded lettuce.

Add 1 of the beef balls to the pan and use a spatula to press very firmly into a thin, flat disc just wider than the bun. Repeat to make a second patty. Season both with salt and pepper and cook for 1–2 minutes, until the edges are browned, the tops are starting to lose their pinkness and the underside is well browned. Flip them over, season with salt and pepper and top with a slice of cheese. Cook for another minute or so, until browned on both sides. Place one patty on top of the other and transfer to your prepared bun base. Repeat this step to make a second burger. If you have a large enough pan, the two burgers can be cooked at the same time.

To serve, top with some sliced pickles, a little more burger sauce and the bun 'lids'. Serve immediately.

Sage and Onion Buttermilk Biscuits

MAKES 4

Made with ingredients that remind me of Irish soda bread but made with a technique that reminds me more of British scones, American buttermilk biscuits are a favourite quick and easy snack. This version, made with sage and onion, is delightful when simply split open and spread with salted butter, but it also makes a fantastic base for a Christmas sandwich filled with leftover ham or turkey, cranberry sauce and maybe even a little gravy.

175g (6oz/1⅓ cups + 1 tablespoon) plain (all-purpose) flour, plus extra for dusting

1 tablespoon baking powder

¼ teaspoon bicarbonate of soda (baking soda)

¼ teaspoon fine sea salt

65g (2½oz/4 tablespoons + 1 teaspoon) unsalted butter, diced and chilled

100ml (3½fl oz/⅓ cup + 4 teaspoons) buttermilk

1 large egg yolk, beaten (optional)

FOR THE SAGE AND ONION

30g (1oz/2 tablespoons) unsalted butter

1 onion, diced

2 tablespoons dried sage

Pinch of fine sea salt

First make the sage and onion mixture. Melt the butter in a frying pan (skillet) over a low–medium heat. Add the onion, sage and salt and cook for about 10 minutes or so, stirring occasionally, until the onion is soft and translucent but not browned. Transfer to a small bowl and set aside until cold.

Place the flour, baking powder, bicarbonate of soda and salt in a large bowl and stir to combine. Add the butter, toss to coat, then press into flat flakes and rub in very lightly, leaving it mainly in large chunks. Place the bowl in the freezer for 10 minutes to harden the butter.

Drizzle in the buttermilk while stirring with a round-tipped knife to form clumps of dough. Now use your hands to gently press the mixture together into a dough.

Line a baking tray (cookie sheet) with parchment paper. Lightly flour a work surface and place the dough on it. Shape into a rectangle, then roll out until it measures 20 x 25cm (8 x 10in). Fold into thirds, like a letter. Cut in half widthways to form 2 equal squares, then stack them on top of one another. Roll out again, but this time into a square roughly 10–15cm (4–6in) wide. Place on the prepared tray and freeze for 15 minutes.

Meanwhile, preheat the oven to 220ºC (200ºC Fan) 425ºF, Gas Mark 7.

Using a sharp knife, cut the chilled square into 4 smaller squares. (If you'd like the biscuits to puff up and expand as much as possible, trimming the edges of the large square before cutting into 4 will help to expose the layers.) Return the squares to the tray, placing them 2cm (¾ in) apart and brush with the beaten egg yolk (if using), or with extra buttermilk if you prefer.

Bake for 13–15 minutes, or until golden brown. Set aside to cool for a few minutes before serving.

I like to serve these still a little warm, but they can be stored in a sealed container and served up to 3 days later.

Cacio e Pepe Stuffed Rolls

MAKES 6

I could eat pasta seven nights a week. There are so many variations of shape, style and flavour that I would never get bored. These bread rolls are inspired by one of my favourite pasta recipes – cacio e pepe, literally 'cheese and pepper', a classic of Roman cuisine. The filling of these buns is made with ricotta, mozzarella and Parmesan, not the cheeses found in the classic pasta dish, but they create a great cheesy filling. The buns are also seasoned with lots of black pepper, but you can halve the amount if you don't want such a strong flavour. Apart from tasting fantastic in their own right, these rolls would also be great served with a tomato-based pasta dish, so long as a carb coma is something you're okay with in your immediate future.

1 batch Brioche Dough (see page 158)

Flour, for dusting

1 large egg, beaten

1 tablespoon melted butter

FOR THE FILLING

100g (3½oz/⅓ cup + 2 tablespoons) ricotta cheese

50g (1¾oz/scant ½ cup) grated mozzarella cheese

25g (1oz/scant ¼ cup) freshly grated Parmesan cheese, plus extra for sprinkling

1 tablespoon freshly ground black pepper, or to taste

Divide the brioche dough into 6 equal pieces and roll into balls. Cover with a clean tea towel (dishtowel) and allow to rest for 10 minutes.

Meanwhile, place the filling ingredients in a bowl and mix together. Set aside.

Line a rimmed 23 x 15cm (9 x 6in) baking tray (eighth sheet pan) with parchment paper. Lightly flour a work surface and roll each ball of dough into a circle about 12cm (5in) in diameter. Divide the filling equally between the circles, then fold the dough up and over the filling, pinching together to form a ball. Place on the prepared tray, cover loosely with clingfilm (plastic wrap) and set aside for 1–1½ hours, or until almost doubled in size.

When ready, preheat the oven to 190ºC (170ºC Fan) 375ºF, Gas Mark 5. Brush the risen buns with beaten egg and bake for about 20 minutes, or until golden. Allow to cool for a few minutes, before brushing with the melted butter and sprinkling with a little extra Parmesan.

These buns are best served while warm so that the cheese is still gooey. You can also store them in a sealed container in the refrigerator for a couple days, reheating them at 180ºC (160ºC Fan) 350ºF, Gas Mark 4 for about 10 minutes.

Cheese-Stuffed Garlic Flatbreads

MAKES 4

Yogurt-based flatbreads, made without yeast, are brilliant — the quickest form of bread you can make, and so versatile. In this recipe they have a mozzarella filling and are brushed with garlic butter, which makes for a fabulous version of garlic bread.

175g (6oz/1⅓ cups + 1 tablespoon) plain (all-purpose) flour, plus extra for dusting

½ teaspoon baking powder

½ teaspoon fine sea salt

175g (6oz/scant ¾ cup) natural yogurt

120g (4¼oz/1 cup) grated mozzarella cheese

Dried chilli flakes, for sprinkling

FOR THE GARLIC BUTTER

100g (3½oz/7 tablespoons) unsalted butter

2 garlic cloves, crushed

Handful of fresh flat leaf parsley, chopped

½ teaspoon sea salt flakes

First make the garlic butter: place the butter in a small pan over a medium heat. Add the crushed garlic and heat until the butter starts to simmer. Pour into a small bowl and refrigerate until the butter starts to firm up, then mix in the parsley and salt.

To make the bread dough, place the flour, baking powder and salt in a large bowl and mix to combine. Make a well in the centre, pour in the yogurt and stir together with a knife. Once clumps start to form, use your hands to bring the mixture together into a soft dough. Knead for a few minutes until smooth, then set aside for 30 minutes.

Cut the dough into 4 equal pieces. Generously flour a work surface and roll each piece into a circle roughly 20cm (8in) in diameter. Sprinkle the middle with the cheese, forming it into a circle roughly 10cm (4in) in diameter. Fold the uncovered dough over the cheese, pinching the seams together to seal it inside. Roll out again, this time into a circle roughly 15cm (6in) in diameter.

Preheat a heavy-based frying pan over a medium heat. When hot, add the flatbreads one at a time and cook for 1–2 minutes, or until the underside is well browned. Flip and cook the other side until browned. Transfer to a serving plate, brush liberally with the garlic butter and sprinkle with a pinch of chilli flakes.

The flatbreads are best eaten on the day they are made, but can be reheated up to a day or two later.

Spiced Cheddar Cornbread Muffins

MAKES 6

There is no better accompaniment to a big, hearty bowl of chilli than a cornbread muffin fresh from the oven; and if it can't be fresh, it's also good toasted and spread with salted butter. The warmth of these muffins comes from smoked paprika, mustard powder and chilli flakes. And, of course, there is Cheddar, because almost everything is better with cheese.

75g (2¾oz/⅔ stick) unsalted butter, melted, plus extra for greasing

75g (2¾oz/⅓ cup + 2 tablespoons) plain (all-purpose) flour

75g (2¾oz/½ cup) fine cornmeal

50g (1¾oz/¼ cup) caster (superfine or granulated) sugar

1 teaspoon baking powder

1 teaspoon English mustard powder

1 teaspoon smoked paprika

¼ teaspoon fine sea salt

2 large eggs, lightly beaten

75ml (2¾fl oz/¼ cup + 1 tablespoon) buttermilk

50g (1¾oz/scant ½ cup) grated strong Cheddar cheese

TO GARNISH

Pickled jalapeño chillies, sliced

Dried chilli flakes

TO SERVE (OPTIONAL)

Warmed honey, for brushing

Finely grated Cheddar cheese, for sprinkling

Preheat the oven to 180°C (160°C Fan) 350°F, Gas Mark 4. Lightly grease a 6-hole muffin tray with a little melted butter.

Place the flour in a large bowl and whisk in the cornmeal, sugar, baking powder, mustard powder, paprika and salt. Make a well in the centre and pour in the eggs, buttermilk and melted butter. Stir together until a smooth batter forms. Add the cheese and stir briefly to combine. Spoon the batter into the prepared tin and top each muffin with a couple of pickled jalapeño slices and a pinch of chilli flakes.

Bake for about 15 minutes, or until the muffins spring back to a light touch. Set aside to cool for a few minutes, before transferring to a wire rack to cool completely.

Before serving, I like to brush the top of the muffins with a little warmed honey and add a sprinkle of extra Cheddar, but this is optional.

The muffins are best served while still warm from the oven. If serving at a later date, store in a sealed container for 2–3 days. In this case, they are best split in half and toasted before being spread with a little salted butter. The muffins also freeze well, but this is best done before the honey and extra Cheddar are added.

NOTE These muffins are on the small side, so if you want to make them larger, line 4 compartments in the muffin tray with paper cases instead of brushing all 6 with butter. The larger size will need to be baked for 17–18 minutes.

Olive Oil and Feta Quickbread

MAKES 4 SERVINGS

A leisurely lunch with my partner while on holiday in Crete provided the inspiration for this savoury loaf. It was the end of the lunch service and we were the only people sitting in a beautiful courtyard enjoying a procession of small dishes. The one that stuck in my memory was baked gigantes beans swimming in beautiful local olive oil flavoured with tomatoes and oregano. We ate every morsel, soaking up the oil with chunks of crusty bread dipped greedily into the most delicious roasted garlic dip.

80ml (3fl oz/⅓ cup) extra virgin olive oil, plus extra for greasing

100g (3½oz/⅔ cup + 2 tablespoons) plain (all-purpose) flour

50g (1¾oz/⅓ cup) cornmeal

1½ teaspoons baking powder

¼ teaspoon bicarbonate of soda (baking soda)

Pinch of fine sea salt

1 tablespoon dried oregano, plus extra for sprinkling

¼ teaspoon dried chilli flakes, plus extra for sprinkling

2 large eggs

60ml (2¼fl oz/¼ cup) whole milk

100g (3½oz/⅔ cup) crumbled feta cheese

1 tablespoon sesame seeds

FOR THE ROASTED GARLIC

1 head of garlic

Fine sea salt

Olive oil

Preheat the oven to 200ºC (180ºC Fan) 400ºF, Gas Mark 6.

Start by making the roasted garlic: discard the outer loose papery skin of the garlic head, leaving the cloves themselves intact. Take a 5–10mm (¼–½in) slice off the top of the head to partially expose the cloves. Place on a piece of foil, sprinkle with salt and drizzle with about 1 tablespoon of oil. Wrap the foil around the garlic and bake for 50–70 minutes, or until the cloves are caramelized and soft. Set aside to cool before squeezing out the garlic. Mash into a paste with a fork and set aside.

Lower the oven temperature to 180ºC (160ºC Fan) 350ºF, Gas Mark 4. Lightly grease a 23 x 13cm (9 x 5in) loaf tin, and line it with a strip of parchment paper that overhangs the long sides, securing it in place with metal binder clips.

Place the flour in a large bowl, add the cornmeal, baking powder, bicarbonate of soda, salt, oregano and chilli flakes and whisk together. Put the eggs, oil, milk and roasted garlic in a jug and whisk together. Make a well in the flour mixture and pour in the eggs. Add half the feta and mix gently with a spatula to form a batter with no visible dry ingredients.

Scrape the batter into the prepared tin and spread evenly. Sprinkle with the reserved feta, followed by the sesame seeds, the extra chilli flakes and a little extra oregano. Bake for 30–35 minutes, or until a skewer inserted into the centre of the loaf comes out clean. Set aside to cool for 15 minutes, before transferring to a wire rack to cool completely.

If stored in a sealed container, the loaf will keep for 2 days, but if sliced and frozen, it is good for up to a month.

Pizza Night for Two

MAKES 2 SERVINGS

My favourite style of pizza, Neapolitan, requires a slowly risen dough and a very high oven temperature. The latter isn't a problem if you have an outdoor pizza oven, but there's no way the average domestic oven can reach the dizzy heights of 500°C (932°F). The way around this is to cook the pizza in a heavy-based frying pan (skillet), which gives great results. Please note that if you do use a domestic oven, it is best to avoid using fresh mozzarella or you'll end up with a very wet pizza. Look for blocks of low-moisture mozzzarella, now widely available in supermarkets.

275g (2¼ cups) '00' pizza flour (11–12% protein content), plus extra for dusting

1g (⅓ teaspoon) fast-action dried yeast

5g (⅛oz/1 teaspoon) fine sea salt

170ml (5¾fl oz/⅔ cup + 2 teaspoons) lukewarm water

Olive oil, for greasing

FOR THE TOPPINGS

200g (7oz) canned plum tomatoes

½ teaspoon fine sea salt

150g (5½oz) low-moisture mozzarella cheese, diced

Other toppings of your choice (I like to add a sprinkling of oregano and chilli flakes, plus a generous amount of pepperoni)

NOTE If you want to freeze the dough for future use, do this as soon as it is halved and rolled into balls. Place them in small individual containers that have been brushed with a little olive oil, then set aside at room temperature for 1 hour, before transferring to the freezer. When you want to use the frozen dough, transfer the containers to the refrigerator overnight, then allow to come to room temperature for 2 hours before needed.

Place the flour, yeast and salt in a large bowl and stir to combine. Make a well in the centre, pour in the water and mix to form a shaggy dough. Tip onto a work surface and knead for 5 minutes or so. Return the dough to the bowl, cover with clingfilm (plastic wrap) and set aside for 15 minutes. Knead again for 5 minutes, or until smooth and elastic. Return to the bowl, cover again and set aside until it has doubled in size, about 4 hours.

Lightly oil a baking tray (cookie sheet). Tip the dough onto a work surface, cut in half and roll each piece into a ball. Place on the prepared tray, cover with clingfilm and set aside for 1 hour, before refrigerating for 12–24 hours. A couple of hours before needed, remove the dough from the refrigerator to bring it to room temperature.

Preheat your grill (broiler) to its highest setting. Place a large frying pan (skillet), preferably cast iron, over a medium–high heat.

Meanwhile, crush the tomatoes in a bowl to form a sauce, then stir in the salt. Set aside.

Generously flour a work surface. Use a dough scraper to transfer a ball from the tray to the floured surface, then use your fingertips to press the dough flat, leaving a slightly raised border around the edge. Gently stretch the dough until you have a pizza base roughly 25–30cm (10–12in) in diameter.

When the frying pan is very hot, carefully drape the pizza base inside it. The dough should start to puff up immediately, so you now need to work quickly. Spoon some of the tomato sauce onto the centre of the pizza, spreading it out to cover the base, but leaving the raised edge clear. Sprinkle over the cheese and any other toppings you fancy. Continue cooking the pizza until the base starts to show signs of browning – this will take just a minute or two. Now place the pan under the grill and cook until the cheese has melted and the crust is starting to brown. Carefully slide the pizza onto a plate and serve immediately.

SMALL BATCH BASICS

Sweet Pastry

MAKES ENOUGH FOR 8 SMALL TARTS

Homemade sweet pastry is always better than shop-bought, and it's also very quick to make. This simple recipe is my go-to for crisp and buttery tarts, perfect for filling with custards, ganaches and all manner of delicious things. Although it makes enough for 8 individual tarts, it's well worth making a full batch as it freezes brilliantly and you then have a great shortcut next time you want homemade pastry.

265g (9½oz/2 cups + 2 tablespoons) plain (all-purpose) flour

40g (1½oz/⅓ cup) icing (powdered) sugar

¼ teaspoon fine sea salt

170g (6oz/1½ sticks) unsalted butter, diced and chilled

1 large egg yolk

¼ teaspoon vanilla bean paste

1 tablespoon ice-cold water

Place the flour, icing sugar and salt in a large bowl and stir to combine. Add the butter and toss to coat, then rub in with your fingertips until the mixture resembles fine breadcrumbs. Add the egg yolk, vanilla and water and use a round-tipped knife to stir them into the flour. Once clumps start to form, use your hands to bring the mixture together into a dough. If it seems dry and crumbly, you can add more water a little at a time to get the correct consistency.

(To save time, the dough can be made in a food processor fitted with a blade attachment. Add the dry ingredients to the processor and pulse to combine. Add the butter and pulse until the mixture resembles fine breadcrumbs. Add the yolk, vanilla and water and pulse just until the mixture starts to clump together.)

Tip the dough onto a work surface and use your hands to quickly bring it together in a uniform ball. Form it into a thick sausage, wrap in clingfilm (plastic wrap) and refrigerate for 1–2 hours, until firm.

At this stage I tend to slice the pastry and freeze the pieces I am not planning to use in the next day or so. If wrapped in clingfilm and stored in the refrigerator, the pastry will keep for 3–4 days, and in the freezer for up to a month.

RECIPES REQUIRING SWEET PASTRY

QUARTER BATCH

Matcha Cheesecake Tarts (see page 29)

HALF BATCH

Egg Custard Tarts (see page 16)
Rhubarb Raspberry Frangipane Tarts (see page 18)
Brown Butter Salted Maple Tarts (see page 26)

Flaky Pastry

MAKES ENOUGH FOR 8 SMALL TARTS

When I want a shatteringly flaky pastry, this is the recipe I use. The vodka it includes is optional, but it does help to hydrate the dough while developing a little less gluten than when using all water. To ensure it has that characteristic flakiness, it's important to keep the butter in large pieces. If you want to make enough for just four tarts (the number most used in this book), you can halve the recipe, but it is easier to make the full batch and keep the remainder for another use.

300g (10½oz/2⅓ cups + 1 tablespoon) plain (all-purpose) flour, plus extra for dusting

1 teaspoon fine sea salt

2 tablespoons caster (superfine or granulated) sugar

250g (9oz/2 sticks + 1½ tablespoons) unsalted butter, diced into 1cm (½in) cubes and chilled

6 tablespoons ice-cold water

2 tablespoons vodka (optional)

Place the flour, salt and sugar in a large bowl and stir to combine. Add the butter and toss to coat, then use your fingertips to press it into flat pieces. Place the bowl in the freezer for 15 minutes.

Mix the ice-cold water with the vodka (or 2 extra tablespoons water if you don't want to use the alcohol). Drizzle some of the liquid into the chilled ingredients, tossing with your hands to distribute. Repeat with the remaining liquid, until a dough starts to form. Use your hands to gently bring the dough together in a ball. Press it into a flat rectangle, wrap in clingfilm (plastic wrap) and refrigerate for 30 minutes.

Lightly flour a work surface and roll the pastry into a rectangle about 15 x 45cm (6 x 18in). Cut into 4 equal pieces, stack them on top of each other and press or roll into a flat rectangle again. Wrap in clingfilm and refrigerate for another 30 minutes.

Reflour the work surface and again roll the pastry into 15 x 45cm (6 x 18in) rectangle. Roll it up like a Swiss roll, wrap in clingfilm and refrigerate overnight, or for at least 1 hour.

The pastry will keep in the refrigerator for 2–3 days, or can be frozen for up to a month.

NOTE If you want a richer, deeper flavour to the pastry, you can replace a third of the plain (all-purpose) flour with another type, such as wholemeal (wholewheat) or rye.

RECIPES REQUIRING FLAKY PASTRY

Choux Pastry

MAKES 4 SERVINGS

The classic formula for choux pastry is easy to remember, being based on the ratios 2:1:1:2 – two parts liquid, one part flour, one part butter and two parts egg. This ratio is by weight, so in this small batch recipe the egg ratio is equivalent to one large egg, weighed out of the shell. If making a larger batch, you can simply weigh the egg to keep the ratio the same as the other ingredients. The pastry is quite straightforward to make, but please read the recipe thoroughly to give yourself the best start.

35g (1¼oz/¼ cup + 1 teaspoon) plain (all-purpose) flour

35ml (1¼fl oz/2 tablespoons + 1 teaspoon) water

35ml (1¼fl oz/2 tablespoons + 1 teaspoon) whole milk

¼ teaspoon caster (superfine or granulated) sugar

¼ teaspoon fine sea salt

35g (1¼oz/2 tablespoons + 1 teaspoon) unsalted butter

1 large egg

Sift the flour into a small bowl and set aside. Place the water, milk, sugar, salt and butter in a small saucepan over a low heat, stirring occasionally until the butter has melted. Increase the heat to medium and bring to a rolling boil. Take the pan off the heat, tip in the flour and stir immediately with a wooden spoon to form a dough. Return the pan to the heat and stir constantly for 1–2 minutes, or until the dough forms a skin on the bottom of the pan (if you like baking science, the finished dough should be around 74–79°C/165–174°F). Tip the pastry into a bowl and beat for a few minutes until cooled slightly, as you don't want to cook the egg in the next step.

Add the egg and beat into the pastry until fully incorporated. The finished texture should be smooth with a slight gloss, and when allowed to fall off the spoon, should form a V-shaped ribbon.

The pastry can be used immediately, but tends to be a little easier to pipe if chilled for an hour or two.

RECIPES REQUIRING CHOUX PASTRY

FULL BATCH

Strawberries and Cream Eclairs (see page 32)
Hazelnut Profiteroles (see page 106)

TIPS FOR WORKING WITH CHOUX

While each use of choux pastry in this book bakes for a different time, you can use the following tips to ensure success whenever you use it.

PIPING

Choux maintains the shape in which it is piped, so it's a good idea to smooth out any peaks or irregularities with a finger dipped in water.

BAKING

Many recipes like to start the baking at a high temperature and lower it after a few minutes, but I find this faffy. I prefer to bake my choux at a constant 190ºC (170ºC Fan) 375ºF, Gas Mark 5. Once the specified time is up, I turn off the oven and allow the choux to cool down inside it. This ensures the pastry stays crisp and won't collapse.

GLAZING

If I am baking choux pastry naked, that is without a topping such as chopped nuts, I do not brush it with beaten egg. This is simply because the choux will brown without it, and there are other options that actually help it to bake better. Once piped, I like to mist it with water, then dust it with a fine layer of icing (powdered) sugar. You can also just spray with a fine mist cake release spray for a similar effect, which browns a little less than a water/sugar combo. Both methods help the choux to open up fully inside, which in turn helps to prevent cracking. Any sugar dusted over the pastry will also caramelize as it bakes, browning it further.

Brioche Dough

MAKES 6 SERVINGS

Traditional brioche is a golden, tender bread rich in butter and eggs. This recipe is a tad lighter on the enriching ingredients to make the dough a little more multifunctional, but don't think it is lacking in any way; it's still a delicious, butter-rich delight.

250g (9oz/2 cups) strong white bread flour

½ teaspoon fine sea salt

1 teaspoon fast-action dried yeast

15g (½oz/1 tablespoon) caster (superfine or granulated) sugar

125ml (4fl oz/½ cup + 1 teaspoon) whole milk

1 large egg

50g (1¾oz/3 tablespoons + 1 teaspoon) unsalted butter, at room temperature, diced

If using a stand mixer, place the flour, salt, yeast and sugar in the bowl and whisk briefly to combine. Make a well in the centre and add the milk and egg. With the dough hook attached, mix to form a shaggy dough. Continue mixing/kneading on a low–medium speed for about 10 minutes, until the dough is smooth and elastic and forms a ball around the hook. Add the butter a couple of pieces at a time and continue mixing until the dough is smooth and elastic and is no longer sticking to the sides or bottom of the dough.

If making the dough by hand, follow the steps above, but rub the butter into the flour mixture before adding the milk and egg. Knead by hand for 15 minutes, or until the dough is smooth and elastic.

Form the dough into a ball and place in a large bowl. Cover with clingfilm (plastic wrap) and refrigerate overnight. If intending to use only half the batch the next day, form the dough into two balls before refrigerating. The unused dough will keep in the refrigerator for up to 3 days.

RECIPES REQUIRING BRIOCHE DOUGH

FULL BATCH

Strawberry Maritozzi (see page 120)
Chocolate and Espresso Brioche Buns (see page 123)
Rhubarb and Marzipan Cream Buns (see page 124)
Cacio e Pepe Stuffed Rolls (see page 140)
Dulce de Leche Pain Suisse (see page 118)
Everything Bagel Morning Buns (see page 126)

ONE-THIRD BATCH

Smash Burgers (see page 136)

VARIATION

To make an even lighter version of the brioche dough, which produces fluffier bread that stays fresher for longer, you can use the Chinese *tangzhong* method (*yukone* in Japanese). Simply place 20g (¾oz) of the flour and 80ml (3fl oz/ ⅓ cup) of the milk in a small saucepan over a medium heat and stir constantly until the mixture gelatinizes and forms a thick paste. Transfer to a bowl and add to the recipe opposite when the remaining milk is added.

BRIOCHE BUNS

These are great for burgers, and the tangzhong method on the left makes for incredibly light buns. Divide the dough into 6 equal pieces, roll into balls and place on a parchment-lined baking tray (cookie sheet). Cover lightly with clingfilm (plastic wrap) and set aside for 1–1½ hours, or until almost doubled in size.

Preheat the oven to 190ºC (170ºC Fan) 375ºF, Gas Mark 5. Lightly brush the buns with beaten egg and bake for 15 minutes, or until golden brown. Set aside to cool completely if using for burgers. In this case, I like to place the buns in a sealed plastic bag while still warm so they steam and the crust softens.

These buns are best used within a couple of days, but they freeze brilliantly, which is really handy if you don't need the whole batch straight away.

Pastry Cream

**MAKES ENOUGH TO FILL
4 INDIVIDUAL TART CASES**

Also known as crème pâtissière, pastry cream is a foundational building block of baking, used in so many recipes that it is well worth learning how to make. It is a classic filling for a fruit tart, but can also be used to fill cakes and pastries, or even folded together with cream to make the dreamiest of mixtures. It keeps well in the refrigerator, so if you think you'll need lots, you can very easily double the ingredients.

300ml (10fl oz/1¼ cups) whole milk

1 teaspoon vanilla bean paste

100g (3½oz/½ cup) caster (superfine or granulated) sugar

25g (1oz/3 tablespoons) cornflour (cornstarch)

4 large egg yolks

30g (1oz/2 tablespoons) unsalted butter, diced

Pinch of fine sea salt

Place the milk, vanilla and half the sugar in a saucepan and bring to a simmer over a medium–high heat, stirring occasionally.

Meanwhile, place the remaining sugar in a bowl with the cornflour and whisk to combine. Add the egg yolks and whisk until smooth.

Once the milk is simmering, pour it over the egg mixture, whisking constantly so that the eggs do not scramble. Return the custard to the pan and place over the same medium–high heat as before, whisking constantly until very thick. Allow to bubble for a minute or so to cook out the cornflour.

Pour the custard into a bowl, add the butter and stir until fully combined. Press a sheet of clingfilm (plastic wrap) directly onto the surface and refrigerate until needed. It will keep for up to a week.

When you're ready to use it, beat the chilled pastry cream until smooth. If there are any lumps, you can pass it through a fine mesh sieve.

**RECIPES REQUIRING
PASTRY CREAM**

HALF BATCH
Blueberry Cream Tarts (see page 21)
Dulce de Leche Pain Suisse (see page 118)

Lemon Curd

MAKES 1 X 400G (14OZ) JAR

A world away from standard lemon curd, this is an incredibly rich and creamy curd made with a slightly unusual method. Inspired by French pastry chefs, such as Pierre Hermé and Jacques Genin, this recipe is brilliant both as a lemon curd but also as a tart filling because, once chilled, it becomes thick enough to hold its shape.

75g (2¾oz/¼ cup + 2 tablespoons) caster (superfine or granulated) sugar

Zest of 2 lemons

75ml (2¾fl oz/¼ cup + 1 tablespoon) lemon juice

1 large egg, plus 1 large yolk

115g (4oz/1 stick) unsalted butter, diced and at room temperature

Place the sugar and lemon zest in a heatproof bowl and rub together with your fingertips until the mixture feels like damp sand and is intensely fragrant. Add the lemon juice, egg and egg yolk and stir together with a whisk. You want to keep everything moving, but without whisking in too much air. Transfer this mixture to a small saucepan over a low–medium heat and stir constantly until it has thickened and reached 75–80ºC (167–176ºF) on an instant-read thermometer. Pour into a measuring jug and set aside for 15 minutes.

Add the butter a little at a time, using a stick blender to combine. This method ensures it is emulsified rather than simply melted into the curd, and gives a thick, luscious texture. Spoon the finished curd into a sterilized jar (see below), seal, label and date, and refrigerate until needed. If unopened, it will keep for 2 weeks.

TIP To sterilize a jam jar, preheat the oven to 140ºC (120ºC Fan) 275ºF, Gas Mark 1. Wash the jar and lid in hot, soapy water and rinse well. Place the jar on a baking tray (cookie sheet) in the oven for about 10 minutes, until completely dry. Place the lid in a bowl of boiling water for a few minutes, then allow to dry.

Fruit Jam

MAKES 1 X 400G (14OZ) JAR

Whenever I have leftover fruit, and there is nothing else I fancy making with it, I will invariably use it to make jam. Below are my two go-to recipes for raspberry and strawberry jam, both great for spreading on my morning toast, but also brilliant for baking purposes, such as sandwiching cakes together, swirling into whipped cream or filling biscuits.

FOR RASPBERRY JAM

300g (10½oz) raspberries

240g (8¾oz/1 cup + 3 tablespoons) caster (superfine or granulated) sugar

FOR STRAWBERRY JAM

300g (10½oz) strawberries, hulled and diced

240g (8¾oz/1 cup + 3 tablespoons) caster (superfine or granulated) sugar

Juice of ½ lemon

EXTRA FLAVOURINGS (OPTIONAL)

1 teaspoon vanilla bean paste, for the strawberry jam

2 teaspoons rose water, for the raspberry jam

To make either jam, place the fruit and sugar in a bowl. Add the lemon juice if making strawberry jam and mix to combine. If making raspberry jam, crush the fruit slightly with a spatula as you mix. Set aside for 30–60 minutes, or until the fruit has released lots of juice.

Place 2 small plates in the freezer. Sterilize a 400g (14oz) jam jar and lid (see page 162).

Transfer the fruit mixture to a saucepan over a high heat and bring to the boil. Continue boiling and stirring for about 5 minutes, or until the mixture reaches 105°C (221°F) on an instant-read thermometer. To test without a thermometer, turn off the heat and spoon a teaspoon of the jam onto one of the chilled plates. Chill for a couple minutes, then push your finger through the jam: if it wrinkles and doesn't flow back together, it is ready; if not, return it to the boil for another minute, then test again.

Once the jam is ready, take the pan off the heat and stir in any additional flavourings you like. Pour the jam into the sterilized jar, then seal, label and date. If unopened, it will keep in the refrigerator for 2 months. Once opened, the jam needs to be used within a month.

Resources

General Bakeware
- Divertimenti https://www.divertimenti.co.uk
- Williams Sonoma https://www.williams-sonoma.com

Eighth Sheet Pan
- Nordicware https://www.nordicware.com

Flour
- Doves Farm Flour https://www.dovesfarm.co.uk
- King Arthur Baking https://www.kingarthurbaking.com

Vanilla Products
- Heilala www.heilalavanilla.com

Tahini
- Belazu www.belazu.co.uk
- Seed and Mill www.seedandmill.com

Chocolate
- Guittard https://www.guittard.com
- Pump St Chocolate https://pumpstreetchocolate.com
- Islands Chocolate https://islandschocolate.com

Matcha
- Japan Centre https://www.japancentre.com
- Kenko Matcha https://kenkomatcha.com

Spices
- Rooted Spices https://rootedspices.com
- Diaspora Co https://www.diasporaco.com

About Edd

Edd Kimber is a baker and food writer based in London.
He is the author of *The Boy Who Bakes* (2011), *Say It With Cake* (2012), *Patisserie Made Simple* (2014), *One Tin Bakes* (2020) and *One Tin Bakes Easy* (2021). Over the last ten years he has appeared on multiple television shows including *Good Morning America*, *The Alan Titchmarsh Show*, *Sunday Brunch*, *Saturday Kitchen* and, of course, on the original series of *The Great British Bake Off*, of which he is the inaugural winner. He regularly shares his knowledge at cookery schools and at food festivals around the world and also writes for multiple UK and international publications.

@THEBOYWHOBAKES
WWW.THEBOYWHOBAKES.CO.UK

Index

An Hachette UK Company
www.hachette.co.uk

First published in Great Britain in 2022 by
Kyle Books, an imprint of Octopus Publishing Group Limited
Carmelite House
50 Victoria Embankment
London EC4Y 0DZ
www.kylebooks.co.uk
This edition published in 2022

ISBN: 978 1 914239 28 1

Distributed in the US by Hachette Book Group, 1290 Avenue of the Americas,
4th and 5th Floors, New York, NY 10104

Distributed in Canada by Canadian Manda Group, 664 Annette St., Toronto,
Ontario, Canada M6S 2C8

Publishing Director: Judith Hannam
Publisher: Joanna Copestick
Editor: Patricia Burgess
Editorial Assistant: Emma Hanson
Design: Evi O. Studio | Katherine Zhang, Susan Le & Wilson Leung
Photography & Food Styling: Edd Kimber
Proofreader: Sally Somers
Production: Lisa Pinnell

Printed and bound in China

10 9 8 7 6 5 4 3 2 1

Acknowledgements

This book was a labour of lockdowns, written as a response to being stuck at home, just me, Mike and the dog. It's a reflection of the way I baked throughout those years, making recipes that were just for us. I'm of course glad that we're finally coming out of that period but also thankful for this new way of baking, an almost reinvigoration of my love for the craft. This style of baking almost feels like baking did for me when I first became obsessed with butter, sugar, eggs and flour; it's a way to relax, a way to de-stress from a bad day at work and it's also a creative outlet. I really loved working on this book and these recipes, I really hope they resonate with you and give you the same joy they do for me.

Of course my first thank you has to go to my readers, your love of baking has allowed me to pursue my passion and turn it into a career that has now lasted well over a decade. Thank you for the continued support.

A massive thank you to everyone at Kyle Books who worked on this project, especially Judith, Louise, Emma, Vic and Hazel. To Trish for making sure my words make sense, to Evi and team for turning my words and images into a beautifully designed book. To Liz for spreading the word across the pond. Thank you.

To Mike (and Wesley) for continually helping me when I'm stuck for an idea and for tasting and giving feedback as I went stir crazy in the kitchen. You have put up with a manic and messy kitchen for three books over the last three years and I am grateful for the patience you have shown. I promise you I'll take a break from books for a while, a year of peace at least.

Thanks to Ovenly Bakery for allowing me to adapt their incredible peanut butter cookie recipe, to Campbell for letting me adapt his English Muffin recipe and to all the other bakeries and people that have in someway inspired recipes in this book.

I truly hope that you all fall in love with *Small Batch Bakes* the same way I have, the recipes have brought so much joy and I can't wait for them to find a place in your kitchen.

Edd x